PRAISE FOR
THE NAMES OF GOD

This is so much more than a study about the many magnificent names of God. As each lesson unfolds, Melissa provides rich biblical history and teaching, personal stories, thought-provoking questions, and practical life application. Your journey through these pages will take you to a deeper, more intimate place in your walk with God.
—**Wendy Blight**, author and biblical content specialist for Proverbs 31 Ministries

Melissa expertly walks you through Old and New Testament Scriptures to discover the many names of God. Not only will you know Him better, but you'll be equipped to trust Him more as you apply these beautiful truths to the details of your life. This study will inspire you to fall in love with the Bible as you fall in love with God.
—**Heather M. Dixon**, speaker and author of *Renewed: Finding Hope When You Don't Like Your Story* and *Determined: Living Like Jesus in Every Moment*

With warmth and wisdom, Melissa Spoelstra leads women into a deeper understanding of who God is and then shows them how to apply that truth. A fundamental study for anyone wanting to experience the victorious Christian life.
—**Grace Fox**, co-director of International Messenger Canada, author of *Moving From Fear to Freedom: A Woman's Guide to Peace in Every Situation*

Melissa's study on the names of God will help you discover the multifaceted character of God, the deep love of God, and His personal pursuit for your heart.
—**Sharon Jaynes**, best-selling author of *The Power of a Woman's Words: How the Words You Speak Shape the Lives of Others* and *Take Hold of the Faith You Long For: Let Go, Move Forward, Live Bold*

Melissa teaches with clarity without sacrificing theological depth. She walks us through the names of God in a way that causes us to pause and ponder the grandeur and goodness of God. Through this study we encounter the character and attributes of our Creator God and leave with a deep awareness of His presence, which instills hope in our hearts.
—**Joel Muddamalle**, director of Theology and Research, Proverbs 31 Ministries

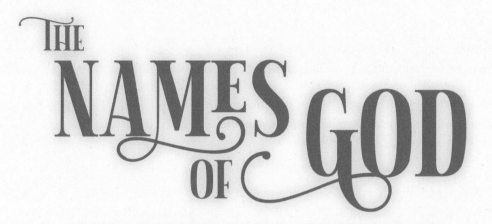

THE NAMES OF GOD

HIS CHARACTER REVEALED

A BIBLE STUDY BY

MELISSA SPOELSTRA

Abingdon Women

Nashville

The Names of God
His Character Revealed

ISBN 978-1-5018-7808-4

20 21 22 23 24 25 26 27 28 29 — 10 9 8 7 6 5 4 3 2 1
MANUFACTURED IN THE UNITED STATES OF AMERICA

CONTENTS

ABOUT THE AUTHOR

Melissa Spoelstra is a popular women's conference speaker (including the Aspire Women's Events), Bible teacher, and author who is madly in love with Jesus and passionate about studying God's Word and helping women of all ages to seek Christ and know Him more intimately through serious Bible study. Having a degree in Bible theology, she enjoys teaching God's Word to the body of Christ, and traveling to diverse groups and churches across the nation and also to Nairobi, Kenya, for a women's prayer conference. Melissa is the author of the Bible studies *Romans: Good News That Changes Everything*, *Elijah: Spiritual Stamina in Every Season*, *Numbers: Learning Contentment in a Culture of More*, *First Corinthians: Living Love When We Disagree*, *Joseph: The Journey to Forgiveness*, and *Jeremiah: Daring to Hope in an Unstable World*, and the books *Dare to Hope*, *Total Family Makeover: 8 Practical Steps to Making Disciples at Home*, and *Total Christmas Makeover: 31 Devotions to Celebrate with Purpose*. She is a regular contributor to the Proverbs 31 First Five App and the Girlfriends in God online daily devotional. She has published articles in *ParentLife*, *Women's Spectrum*, and *Just Between Us* and writes her own regular blog in which she shares her musings about what God is teaching her on any given day. Melissa lives in Pickerington, Ohio, with her pastor husband, Sean, and their four kids: Zach, Abby, Sara, and Rachel.

Follow Melissa:

 @MelSpoelstra

 @Daring2Hope

 @Author MelissaSpoelstra

Her blog MelissaSpoelstra.com
(check here also for event dates and booking information)

INTRODUCTION TO THIS STUDY

If we're honest, sometimes God feels so far away. It can be hard to make sense of injustice and suffering in the world. Other times His instructions in Scripture seem confusing to us. We want to draw near to God and develop a deeper relationship with Him, but we have so many questions about Him. How can we know God better?

One of the ways God makes Himself known to us is through His names in Scripture. While our names help identify and distinguish us, God's names go a step further: *they reveal God to us*. Studying God's names helps us grow in our understanding of His character.

At times our culture—and even other Christians—can give us a distorted view of God. If we aren't careful, we can find ourselves thinking that God exudes qualities He doesn't possess, such as being unloving or apathetic toward His creation. In a world where we find people creating God in their image, studying His names helps us remember that we are created in His. God's names give us a more complete view of Him.

As we dive into studying names such as Elohim, Yahweh, Messiah, and many others, we will journey toward greater intimacy with God. We won't find answers for every question, but we will develop greater trust in the Lord in the midst of life's ambiguities. We'll be reminded that God does not promise continual happiness and ease for His followers but offers something better—a loving relationship that lasts forever!

The first women's Bible study I ever completed was a study of God's names. It helped me to know more about God's character, His interaction with people, and His love for me personally. Over the years I've had many moments when the truths from that study have given me practical help and encouragement. When I've felt alone, I've recalled that God is El Roi, the God who sees me. When I have fretted over unexpected expenses, I have remembered that He is Yahweh Yireh, the God who provides. Other times I have been brought to a place of conviction or worship as I have embraced God's authority as El Elyon or His power as Adonai.

My prayer for you, whether you have been walking with God for many years or are just starting out in your relationship with Him, is that through this study you will not just come to know more about God but will know Him better in an intimate, loving relationship. The more we know Him, the more we will find His heart and learn to trust Him with everyday things such as our relationships, our budgets, and our thought lives. As the psalmist observed, "Those who know your name trust in you, for you, O Lord, do not abandon those who search for you" (Psalm 9:10).

Here's the best part: as we discover God's names, we'll discover H*im*. And as Colossians 1:10b says, "You will grow as you learn to know God better and better." This is our goal!

About the Study

Each day in our study we will focus on 3 Bs:

- **Behold.** As we study God's names, we will behold Him. We will learn about His character, His interactions with people, and His heart attitudes toward His creation—which includes me and you.
- **Believe.** After we behold God, I pray we will move into deeper faith. We will grow in belief as we see Him for who He really is.
- **Bloom.** After we behold and believe God, then we will have a greater understanding of His heart behind His commands. This will impact our thoughts, attitudes, and actions.

At the end of each day's lesson, we will recap what we have beheld, write a statement of what we believe about God in response to the name we studied that day, and identify possible ways our behaviors might be transformed as we consider everyday life situations we are facing.

The order of these steps is important. We can't focus first on the outcomes in our lives. When we do, we risk making our faith about legalistic rituals rather than a personal relationship with our Creator God. So, in our study of God's names we will behold, believe, and then see the Lord transform us as we bloom and exhibit His fruit in our lives.

We will begin our study in Genesis with the name El, spending our first two weeks unpacking Scriptures that mention the various forms of this name for God that highlight His power and personal interest in His creation—names such as Elohim, El Roi, and El Elyon. Then we'll spend another two weeks exploring the name Yahweh, the self-existent One. Scripture includes many combinations of Yahweh with other words that reveal specific character traits of our amazing God, such as Yahweh Rapha, God our healer, and Yahweh Yireh, God our provider. During our fifth week of study we'll look at other names such as Adonai, Abba, and the Holy Spirit of God. Jesus's names will be the focus of our final week together.

Throughout our weeks of study we will see the same God operating in three persons— Father, Son, and Holy Spirit—showing us that the continuity of His character and plan has not changed. Although we still will have questions about God and will have to live with some measure of trust in the things we cannot see or understand, I believe that six weeks of intentionally setting our focus on the character of God will enable us to pray like the psalmist, "Not to us, O Lord, not to us, but to your name goes all the glory for your unfailing love and faithfulness" (Psalm 115:1). May our study move each of us to greater love and worship of our faithful God.

Options for Study

Before beginning the study, I invite you to consider the level of commitment your time and life circumstances will allow. I have found that what I put into a Bible study directly correlates to what I get out of it. When I commit to do the homework daily, God's truths sink deeper as I take time to reflect and meditate on what God is teaching me. When I am intentional about gathering with other women to watch videos and have discussion, I find that this helps keep me from falling off the Bible study wagon midway. Also, making a point to memorize verses and dig deeper by looking at additional materials greatly benefits my soul.

At other times, however, I have bitten off more than I can chew. When our faith is new, our children are small, or there are great demands on our time because of difficult circumstances or challenges, we need to be realistic about what we will be able to finish. So this study is designed with options that enable you to tailor it to your particular circumstances and needs.

1. Basic Study. The basic study includes five daily readings or lessons. Each lesson combines study of Scripture with personal reflection and application (boldface type indicates write-in-the-book questions and activities), ending with a suggestion for talking with God about what you've learned and a "Big Idea," or takeaway, from the lesson. On average you will need about twenty to thirty minutes to complete each lesson.

At the end of each week, you will find a Weekly Wrap-Up to guide you in a quick review of what you've learned. You don't want to skip this part, which you'll find to be one of the most practical tools of the study. This brief exercise will help your takeaways from the lessons to "stick," making a real and practical difference in your daily life.

When you gather with your group to review each week's material, you will watch a video, discuss what you are learning, and pray together. I encourage you to discuss the insights you are gaining and how God is working in your own life.

2. Deeper Study. If you want an even deeper study, there are memory verses for each week, and you'll find a memorization exercise at the end of each lesson.

3. Lighter Commitment. If you are in a season of life in which you need a lighter commitment, I encourage you to give yourself permission to do what you can. God will bless your efforts and speak to you through this study at every level of participation.

Take time now to pray and decide which study option is right for you, and check it on the following page.

___ 1. Basic Study
___ 2. Deeper Study
___ 3. Lighter Commitment: I will_____.

Be sure to let someone in your group know which option you have chosen to do so that you have some accountability and encouragement.

A Final Word

I'm so excited to pursue knowing God on a deeper level alongside you! Would you take a moment now to ask the Lord to help you learn and draw closer to Him through our study of His names? We don't want to just learn facts about God; we want to grow in our relationship with Him. I'm praying that by the time we've turned the last page, we will sense His love and nearness and experience His power and grace in unique and powerful ways!

Melissa

Video Viewer Guide: Introductory Video

You will grow as you learn to know God better and better.
                              (Colossians 1:10)

Each day in our study we will focus on 3 Bs:

B_____

B_____

B_____

The first mention gives us the _____ _____.

Weeks 1 and 2: _____ Names

Weeks 3 and 4: _____ Names

Weeks 5 and 6: The _____

Adonai, Abba, Holy Spirit, Jesus

Jesus: Yahweh is _____

Those who know your name _____ in you,
    for you, O Lord, do not abandon those who search for you.
                              (Psalm 9:10)

Not to us, O Lord, not to us,
        but to your name goes all the _____
        for your unfailing love and faithfulness.
                              (Psalm 115:1)

Week 1

EL (PART 1)

Hashem, Elohim, El Elyon, El Roi

Memory Verse

Honor the LORD for the glory of his name.
Worship the LORD in the splendor of his holiness.
(Psalm 29:2)

Day 1: Hashem—The Name

One of the first things we learn about a person upon meeting him or her is that person's name. Sometimes a surname can help us connect people with their families as we discover they are related in some way. When I got married, I changed my last name to identify with my husband—and later with our children who would bear that name. Recently someone at the place where I exercise told the class that she was getting married and mentioned what her new last name would be. I had never met her officially before, but I recognized the last name. I introduced myself after the workout and found that I knew some of her future family members. Names help us make connections.

The Bible reveals to us that names are significant for other reasons, as well.

Scripture Focus

Exodus 20:7; various psalms; Isaiah 52:6

- God's first assignment to Adam was to name the animals, which helped him to discover his need for human companionship.
- The Lord changed several people's names to mark a transformation in their lives. For example, Jacob's name meant "deceiver," and God changed it to Israel, which means "God prevails" (Genesis 32:28).[1] Similarly, Jesus changed Simon's name to Peter, which means "rock" (Matthew 16:16-18). In Scripture, a change of name reveals a change of identity.
- Parents in biblical times chose names carefully. Sometimes a name was related to a natural object (e.g., Jonah: dove; Tamar: palm tree). Other times the name was related to a time, place, circumstance, or peculiarity of a child.[2] (Jacob's brother was named Esau because he was hairy!)

Today we may or may not be interested in what a name actually means. My parents named me Melissa, which means "honey bee." I think they just liked the sound of it. You may have a family name or a name chosen for its meaning. We named one of our daughters Sara after my husband's sister and another daughter Rachel after one of his cousins.

When we named our son, I was in my last trimester of pregnancy. My husband and I were sitting at a local fast-food place in Canada, where we were living at the time, waiting for a car repair. We had a little book of baby names and went through it page by page. We debated many different names along the way but couldn't come to an agreement. When we finally got to Z and found Zachary, we both liked it. It means "remembered of the Lord."

What is the meaning of your name? If you don't know, you can go to www.behindthename.com or Google it for some historical background and meaning.

My name, _____, means . . .

Extra Insight

In Scripture, the word *name* appears over 1,000 times. While *shem* is the Hebrew word for "name," the New Testament uses the Greek word *onoma*.[3]

One of the gals in the pilot group for this study said her name wasn't listed on any website or found in any book. Her mom had changed a family member's name to create something unique. It doesn't matter whether your name has some special significance or your parents just liked the way it rolled off the tongue—it's special because it was chosen for *you*. Yet whether or not the particular meanings of our names are important to us, what people call us does matter.

It can be infuriating when someone continually refers to us with the wrong name or uses our name and identity. Several years ago, someone used my name to purchase five new phones in another state. They stole my name and other information, and it ended up being a pain to sort out. The act of someone using our names for their personal gain is called identity theft.

Names matter, and God clearly communicates in His Word that He is serious about how we use His name.

Shem is the Hebrew word used in the Old Testament to refer to someone's name. When we find the Hebrew word H*ashem*, it means "The Name," which denotes God's name.[4] Throughout our study we will be focusing on God's many names that reveal His character. Through these titles we will find His essence and power. Before we delve into our study of these names, I want us to consider our posture toward God's names.

Read Exodus 20:7 in the margin and circle the repeated word that indicates what we must not do when it comes to God's name.

Many translations say it this way: "You shall not take the name of the LORD your God in vain" (NASB, ESV, NKJV).

What are some ways that God's name can be misused or taken in vain? (Describe one or more scenarios rather than give specific word examples.)

"You must not misuse the name of the LORD your God. The LORD will not let you go unpunished if you misuse his name."

(Exodus 20:7)

Perhaps you thought of when people lightly say, "Oh my..." in front of God's name in casual conversation or as an expletive when they are upset or excited. That certainly can be a misuse of His name, but as we look at the Hebrew word *shav'* we find that here "misuse" means "emptiness, vanity, falsehood."[5] So, to use God's name in vain means that it is empty or without meaning. Dr. Tony Evans describes it this way: "It has to do with using God's name in a way that's inconsistent with His personhood. It involves stripping away the value that belongs to His name.... When God is not understood, valued, and appreciated for who He truly is, using His name is like an identity theft."[6]

Throughout church history we find that people controlled or even abused others using God's name. Joan of Arc was burned at the stake in His name. Wars were fought in His name. Politicians have used His name to push their own agendas. Though these specific examples may not hit close to home for us personally, it is important to consider our own use of God's name. Are there any ways we might be using His name in vain? Do we understand, value, and appreciate God for who He really is when we use His name? We want to think and speak about God in a way that is consistent with what we know to be true about Him from Scripture.

Let's spend some time looking at how some of the psalmists encourage us to use God's name.

Read each verse and circle the verb that is associated with our usage of God's name. Then write an example to show how you might accomplish this practically (answers will vary). I've done the first one for you:

I *will be filled with joy because of you.*
   I *will* (sing) *praises to your name, O Most High.*
                              (Psalm 9:2)

<u>While driving today I can sing a worship song that praises God's name.</u>

Come, let us tell of the LORD's greatness;
   let us exalt his name together.
                    (Psalm 34:3)

_____

_____

I *will bring honor to your name in every generation.*
   Therefore, the nations will praise you forever and ever.
                              (Psalm 45:17)

_____

_____

Extra Insight

Jesus instructed His disciples to pray like this, "Our Father in heaven, / may your name be kept holy" (Matthew 6:9).

Then I called on the name of the LORD:
  "Please, Lord, save me!"
                    (Psalm 116:4)

_____

_____

How we actually put these commands into practice in everyday life can be as simple as singing a song of worship, revering God's name so that we don't use it flippantly, or calling out to God to save us. What we discover in these passages is that we will not misuse God's name when we are praising, honoring, or calling on it. We also found that we can praise God's name together with others. As I've been studying God's name, I have noticed that so many of the songs we sing in worship focus on God's name. I've also found that the psalms are loaded with references to how we are to use God's name. Praise, honor, and worship are the words most associated with *Hashem* throughout the psalms. Let's take a moment to put these commands into practice.

Write a prayer of praise below. You might want to include the song lyrics of a favorite hymn or worship song that talks about God's name.

I want to end our time today with some encouraging verses that remind us that God's name is powerful. It is our place of safety. We can worship knowing our God is worthy of our praise.

Read the following verses and underline the word *name*. Then draw a star by the verse that most resonates with you today:

The LORD says, "I will rescue those who love me.
  I will protect those who trust in my name."
                    (Psalm 91:14)

He has paid a full ransom for his people.
  He has guaranteed his covenant with them forever.
  What a holy, awe-inspiring name he has!
                    (Psalm 111:9)

Not to us, O LORD, not to us,
  but to your name goes all the glory
  for your unfailing love and faithfulness.
                    (Psalm 115:1)

Your name, O Lord, endures forever;
your fame, O Lord, is known to every generation.
(Psalm 135:13)

The name of the Lord is a strong fortress;
the godly run to him and are safe.
(Proverbs 18:10)

"But I will reveal my name to my people, and they will come to know
its power. Then at last they will recognize that I am the one who speaks
to them."

(Isaiah 52:6)

Now take a moment to reread Isaiah 52:6 above.

God reveals His name to us, and through it we can know God's power. Do you want to know God's power? I know I do. I also want to recognize God's voice in my life as I seek to know Him better and discern how to relate to others, manage my finances, and organize my day. God says that we *can* know Him better, experience His power, and hear His voice. That blows my mind! When I read those promises, my desire is not to misuse God's name but to worship the One who bears it.

Application can be a little tricky when it comes to a study such as this one. At the end of each day, there might not be a specific action step we can take. Instead we will be growing a bigger view of God that will impact our worldview. God is revealing Himself to us through His names so that we might know Him. I want that so much. I'm praying you do too.

So, each day we are going to end our time together with three Bs—Behold, Believe, Bloom—to help us soak in the rich truths surrounding God's names. This will be a time to review the name we've studied and write a statement of our belief in the character trait it reveals about God. Then we will look for ways to see that truth take root and bloom in our lives as God transforms us from the inside out.

Behold

God's name is the name above every name (Philippians 2:9). We want His name to be kept holy so that we don't misuse it in any way.

Believe

Write a statement of belief:

Because I believe that God's name is powerful and reveals His

character, I _____.

Bloom

When we behold and believe, God does the work of producing fruit in our lives through His Spirit. Take a moment to consider how the truths we've studied in the Scriptures today might impact your life. What thoughts, attitudes, or actions might change as you embrace these truths?

You don't need to write anything down, but I think it is important to ask yourself this question and listen for promptings of the Holy Spirit. My prayer is that today's introductory lesson will whet your appetite with anticipation as you seek to develop intimacy with God through a study of His names.

Talk with God

Lord, Your name is great and worthy of praise. I long to know You more. Reveal Yourself to me as I study Your names. Help me not to misuse Your name, which represents You. Lord, show me any area where I might be misrepresenting You. Give me a clearer picture of who You are so that I can worship You more intimately. Amen.

Memory Verse Exercise

Big Idea

Our desire is not to misuse God's name but to worship the One who bears it.

Read the Memory Verse on page 12 several times, and then fill in the blanks below as you recite it:

Honor the _____ for the glory of his name.
   Worship the _____ in the splendor of his holiness.
                                                   (Psalm 29:2)

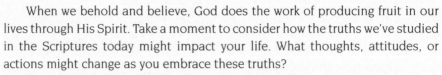

Day 2: Elohim—Creator

Scripture Focus

Genesis 1:1-31

My daughter and I attended a painting party at my friend's house. She had canvases set up all around her dining room table for a group of us to create some art. I've been to similar gatherings before, so I was expecting the instructor to tell us exactly what colors to use, which brushes to choose, and precisely where to put each stroke. I'm not an artist by any stretch of the imagination, but I've found that when someone tells me exactly what to do, I can follow instructions—and it may not turn out half bad.

This leader was different. She made suggestions and gave some directions, but told us we could use any colors or brushes we liked. The picture was of a floral arrangement, which she said could have any type of flowers. We were just supposed to use our creativity. This is where it breaks down for me. I can copy things, but knowing how to create something artistically isn't hard-wired in my brain. My daughter's painting was unique and amazing while mine looked like it belonged in a third-grade art show.

Some of us may embrace our artistic gifts, while others of us feel like we missed out on the creativity gene. Today we are going to study the first name used of God in Scripture, and we are going to find that God is the ultimate Creator. We'll also discover that no one actually lacks the creative gene because God made us in His image.

Take a moment to consider the last thing you created. It might have been a meal, a DIY project, or a design for work. Write about or draw a picture of your last creation below:

While creating through art isn't my place of inspiration, I have created magazine articles and better systems for organizing junk drawers. As we seek to know God better, we find that the very first usage of "God" in Scripture is translated from the Hebrew word E*lohim*, which reveals something about God's creative ability.

Read Genesis 1:1-31 and look for at least five verbs associated with God's first actions in Scripture:

1. _____

2. _____

3. _____

4. _____

5. _____

Depending on your translation, you may have found different forms of words such as these:

- created,
- said,
- saw,
- called,
- made,
- blessed, or
- looked.

Are these the actions of an impersonal force? No, our God did not start the world in motion and then detach Himself from it. These words remind us that He is a personal, loving God. The ancient name E*lohim* is actually a plural form

Extra Insight

The Latin term *ex-nihilo* is often used to refer to God's creative ability to create something from nothing.[7]

of El.[8] El was the term for god borrowed from the Canaanites and could refer to both the true God and pagan gods.[9] It means "mighty" or "strong."[10] So while the name Elohim carries with it the authority and sovereignty of One who is strong, we also find Him to be intensely personal.

Today we want to camp on this truth: Elohim created us, and He only makes good things.

Extra Insight

Elohim is the only word used for God in Genesis 1 and is found over thirty times. It is the word most used for God in the Old Testament, being used over 2,500 times.[11]

Scan back over Genesis 1. How many times does Elohim use the word *good* to describe the things He made?

Reread Genesis 1:26-27 and identify in whose image God created people:

God made us in His own image. While you may not like the texture of your hair, the size of your feet, or your artistic ability, Elohim made you that way. His original design was based on His own image. When we look in the mirror, we see a reflection of our image. We also see a reflection of Elohim's image, hardwired into our DNA.

What if you really were to view yourself as made in the image of God? How would that affect your self-talk and confidence level?

I know that if I kept this in mind, I wouldn't put myself down as much or complain about the things I can't do, such as carry a tune or paint pictures. I'd focus on what God did create in me instead of what He didn't.

Now take a moment to consider how Elohim sees you. Look up the following verses and note what kind of things God sees when He looks at you:

Matthew 10:29-31

2 Corinthians 5:17

Colossians 2:13-14

1 Peter 2:9

1 John 3:1

Among other things, God says in His Word that you are valued, new in Christ, forgiven, chosen, and loved. God made you in His very image, and though sin has corrupted the planet, God found you so valuable that He sent His Son to cleanse and redeem you. In my early years of learning about God, so much of the teaching I received was focused on sin separating us from God. I embraced the notion that it was prideful to acknowledge anything good about myself. Yet I now believe that if Elohim said it was good, we can too!

Write below at least one positive attribute that you possess as a person created in God's image:

It is OK to acknowledge our God-given attributes. The gals in my pilot study group identified their own positive attributes as humor, compassion, encouragement, gentleness, the ability to bake, welcoming neighbors, caring for children, and creative decorating.

Take a moment to write a short prayer thanking God for how He made you.

While much of life doesn't seem very good at times, we can hold on to the knowledge that the original creation was good. Elohim only makes good things.

We need balance as we think about ourselves and others as both those who need Christ to restore our relationship with Elohim and people who are made in the image of God. Every person on the planet was created in the image of God. It grieves Him when we devalue His creation.

What are some ways that we can devalue other people?

We don't want to devalue something God greatly values—the pinnacle of His creation: people. Gossip assaults the image of God in others as we tear them down with words. Judgmental and condescending attitudes also push others down rather than lift them up. Abuse and mistreatment certainly devalue people.

We live in a world where people are aching to hear that they are valued and loved. Since we know that Elohim created every person in His image, may we be the loudest voices asserting the inherent value of every person.

Behold

Today we beheld Elohim, the mighty Creator.

Believe

Write a statement of belief:

I believe that Elohim _____.

Perhaps you said that He made you in His image, created the world, made only good things, or something completely different. Don't overthink this portion. Our goal is to deepen our knowledge of God so that we can draw nearer to Him through His revealed character.

Bloom

Take a moment to think about people in your world. Your family and friends. Your coworkers. The pizza delivery person and the checker at the grocery store. The single mother across the globe struggling to feed her children. The person on social media who annoys you with her strong opinions. Elohim made each of them in His image. When we begin to see ourselves and others this way, our lenses change. We look for the good—that original good—that God saw in everything He made. When we behold God as our Creator and believe that everything He makes is good, we can bloom as we realize the great value of every person on the planet, including us.

Talk with God

Elohim, You are mighty and strong. Nothing is too hard for You. I surrender my family, job, and to-do list into Your hands. Provide me with Your strength. You made me in Your image. Help me remember and appreciate Your creative acts in my life today. Amen.

Memory Verse Exercise

Big Idea

Elohim created us, and He only makes good things.

Read the Memory Verse on page 12 several times, and then fill in the blanks below as you recite it:

Honor the _____ *for the* _____ *of his name.*
   Worship the _____ *in the* _____ *of his holiness.*
                                                      (Psalm 29:2)

Day 3: Elohim—The Strong One

In the past year we've moved from our home where we lived for nineteen years to a new town, so making friends has been a priority for me. While first impressions are important, I've been taking it slow and really trying to get to know people.

Think of someone you know really well. How did you forge a deep relationship with this person?

Scripture Focus

Deuteronomy 10:17; Isaiah 46:9-10; Jeremiah 23:23-24

I thought of my mentor, Deb, whom I've known for over twenty years. We've spent hours talking and have had many shared experiences together, so our relationship is deep and rich. Relationships don't get deep overnight. It takes intentionality and time to develop intimacy with others. As we seek to know God on a deeper level, we find that God revealed Himself over time to His people. He started by showing us He is Elohim, the mighty Creator. Today we continue our study of Elohim in order to glean additional insights into God's character that are revealed in this name.

Elohim is the plural form of El. This leads us to the question, "Why is Elohim plural?" We see plural pronouns used in Genesis 1:26 where Elohim says, "Let us make human beings in our image."

Why do you think God refers to Himself in the plural form here?

It's OK if you said you have no idea! Several different views have been discussed by commentators, but here are three views that rose to the top for me:

1. Trinity—God is expressing glimpses of the Trinity from the beginning.
2. Heavenly Host—God is expressing Himself as plural by including the angelic army alongside Him.
3. Plural of Majesty—Because of His deity and power, God is referred to as plural.[12]

Perhaps you thought of the Trinity. We see the Spirit of God hovering over the waters in Genesis 1:2. The New Testament also sheds more light on the subject.

Read Colossians 1:15-16 below.

15Christ is the visible image of the invisible God.
He existed before anything was created and is supreme over all
creation,
16for through him God created everything
in the heavenly realms and on earth.
He made the things we can see
and the things we can't see—
such as thrones, kingdoms, rulers, and authorities in the unseen world.
Everything was created through him and for him.

(Colossians 1:15-16)

According to these verses, who was involved in Creation?

Extra Insight

"Progressive revelation is a movement from truth to more truth and so to full truth."[13]

We know from the whole Bible that Jesus was a part of Creation. Though Jesus isn't mentioned specifically in Genesis 1, over time God continued to reveal more of Himself to His people, and in the present day we have the ability to see the fullness of God revealed in Scripture. The plural name Elohim holds great meaning for us as Christ-followers since we see glimpses of the triune God from the beginning of time. It makes sense to us that God would reveal Himself as plural since we now know that He consists of three persons including Father, Son, and Holy Spirit.

However, we also must consider how the original audience—the ancient Hebrews—would have understood the text and made sense of the plural name. They didn't have the fullness of revelation that we have with the complete canon of Scripture. The theological term for the way God has revealed Himself over time is "progressive revelation." God gradually has showed us more and more about Himself through His Word, His Son, and His Spirit (Matthew 28:19; John 14:26). Theologians have found that if you look at a verse that dates somewhere in the middle of this progression of revelation, you may miss some of the context of the verse unless you go backward or forward in Scripture. We might say that the Old Testament is the beginning of God's progressive revelation of Himself.

So, how did the ancient Hebrews understand the plural name Elohim? They knew a Messiah was coming, but they didn't know His name and wouldn't have understood that He was present in Creation. They might have associated the plural tense of God's name with His majesty, as this was a common practice in ancient tradition. To ascribe greatness, a deity in ancient times was sometimes referred to in the plural form. Whether or not the plural's sole purpose was to emphasize God's majesty, the meaning of this name certainly tells us about

God's might and strength. We see this in how the name Elohim is used throughout the Old Testament. Let's look at a few Scriptures that emphasize aspects of Elohim's greatness that we can hold on to in our relationship with Him.

Read the following three passages and write a word or phrase that sticks out to you about Elohim beside each one:

Deuteronomy 10:17

Isaiah 46:9-10

Jeremiah 23:23-24

From Deuteronomy 10:17, and many other verses in Scripture, we learn that He is mighty and awesome. Another way to describe this greatness is *omnipotent*, which means all-powerful. This passage basically says our God is the Elohim of elohims. There is nothing that is too difficult for Him!

Isaiah 46:9-10 tells us that our God knows everything. He is *omniscient*. He knows what you have been through in the past, what you are facing today, and all that will come in your future.

From the prophet Jeremiah, we see that Elohim is *omnipresent*. He is everywhere at the same time. While we try to multitask and get a lot of stuff accomplished, we can only be in one place at a time. Can you imagine being able to fold laundry, check homework, and answer emails all at the same time?

From these passages, what do you notice about how different God is from us?

What encourages you about His abilities?

For me, the idea of Elohim being omnipotent (all-powerful), omniscient (all knowing), and omnipresent (everywhere at the same time) is difficult to wrap my mind around. God is not like us. He is set apart. "Set apart" is actually what the word *holy* means. God is not a rock, bird, or person. Those are just things He made. I believe this is why He is so persistent throughout Scripture with warnings about idol worship. God's creation is beautiful and to be appreciated, but it isn't to take His place in our hearts. The word *transcendent* describes holiness well—"going beyond ordinary limits; surpassing; exceeding" or "superior or supreme."[14]

Extra Insight

"Some theologians refer to *Elohim* as the Holy Other, which can be defined as something we are not aware of. Yet a closer look at the names of God constructed from the root word *Elohim* reveals a God who also abides in the realm we know."[15]

At times I reduce God to something I can understand and define, but we can't put the transcendent Elohim in a box. He exists beyond and above us. He is outside of time. He made the beginning and already knows the end. This stretches my brain to its edges. I live by a calendar and a clock. I'll bet you do too.

Knowing God through His name Elohim means accepting that we cannot figure Him out. We can draw near to Him, and He will draw near to us (James 4:8). But we must draw near accepting some level of ambiguity because His strength goes beyond the limits of our finite minds.

If Elohim has the power to speak the world into existence, He can help us today with whatever struggles we are facing. Our Creator is mighty!

Write some of the big and little problems you have encountered recently below:

As I contemplate how incredibly mighty Elohim is, I wonder why I get so freaked out over the struggles of life. When cars get towed, job applications are turned down, and health challenges arise, I'm sometimes tempted to think God either has bigger problems to address or He won't really intervene in my struggles.

How can seeing God's might and power in the name Elohim change your perspective toward your problems right now?

Reconciling the power of God with our real-life problems is one of the reasons I believe it is so important to study His names. It helps us remember who He is. As we continue to study God's many names, we will discover His gentleness, power, peace, and provision. But first things first. God wanted us to know that He is strong. He is not a weak god. He isn't experimenting, manipulating, or clawing His way to power. *Nothing* is impossible for Him!

Behold

Today we have beheld Elohim as the strong One who is omnipotent, omniscient, and omnipresent.

Believe

Write a statement of belief:

I believe Elohim _____.
(Remember that there isn't one right answer!)

Bloom

We can trust Elohim with the big stuff—cancer, job loss, and divorce. We can trust Him with the small stuff—flat tires, overwhelmed schedules, and broken washing machines. There is no perfect life—no perfect job, church, or relationship. But there *is* a perfect God. His name is Elohim.

I hope one of your takeaways from our study of Elohim's name is the knowledge that your God is stronger than any problem you are facing today. He has the power and knowledge to help you. His presence will never leave you. I pray that as you behold and believe your strong Elohim, you will bloom with renewed strength today.

Talk with God

Elohim, You are not like me, yet You have chosen to reveal Yourself to me. That blows my mind! Help me not to reduce You to my human level. You are all powerful, all knowing, and everywhere all the time. God, You are right here with me as I study Your names. Teach me to lean on Your strength when mine is all gone. I want to trust You more today. Amen.

Memory Verse Exercise

Read the Memory Verse on page 12 several times, and then fill in the blanks below as you recite it:

Honor the _____ for the _____ of his _____.
Worship the _____ in the _____ of his _____.
(Psalm 29:2)

Big Idea

Elohim is stronger than any problems we face today.

Day 4: El Elyon—God Most High

Scripture Focus

Genesis 14;
Hebrews 5:9-10;
7:1-3

My daughter's friend faced some pretty significant health challenges in high school. It got so bad at one point that she couldn't raise her hands above her head to even wash her hair. She thought she would never be able to go to

college and take care of herself with the amount of pain she battled on a daily basis.

Through these debilitating setbacks, she set her attention on the Lord, focusing on what she could do more than what she couldn't. Though she felt her setbacks outnumbered her abilities at times, she felt more determined than ever to be able to attend nursing school.

This gal is now my daughter's roommate in college. She still battles pain daily, but she completed her freshman year and presses on against the odds to see her dream of becoming a nurse fulfilled.

Can you think of a time when you were able to accomplish something when the odds were not in your favor? If so, describe it briefly:

Being able to have children when doctors weren't sure I could get pregnant comes to my mind. I know others who got out of debt when it seemed insurmountable. I've had friends who weren't sure they could forgive an infidelity in their marriage and came out with a stronger relationship after years of hard work. Whether our challenges are physical, emotional, mental, or spiritual, many of us have felt as though the odds were stacked against us until we encountered the supernatural help of God.

While every challenge doesn't end up with a storybook ending, we can believe by faith that our God is the most powerful force in the universe. Yesterday we saw that He is Elohim, the Mighty One. We will continue in that vein today as we see that He is also El Elyon, God Most High. El is the same root word found in Elohim. Elyon literally means "supreme God."[16] "When *El* is combined with E*lyon*, the compound connection refers to God as the highest or as the most."[17]

Let's look at the first mention of El Elyon ("God Most High") in Scripture—as we will do for many of the names of God in our study—because the first mention often sets the tone of interpretation. Though this first mention is in Genesis 14:18, we see that a lot has happened on the earth since Elohim spoke the world into existence at the beginning of the book. We find that God called a man named Abram to leave his homeland and travel to a new country, promising that Abram's descendants would be blessed and the entire world would be blessed through him (Genesis 12:2-3). Abram traveled with his family, including a nephew named Lot. When their herdsmen began to squabble, Abram and Lot separated. Abram offered Lot first pick of the land in Canaan, and he chose to pitch his tents near a town named Sodom (Genesis 13:12).

Extra Insight

"Those who study the Bible in a serious way sometimes refer to the Law of First Mention. It's not so much a law, really, as a common principle in the Scriptures. If you select an important biblical word…you'll find that its first biblical appearance sets the tone for all the richness of meaning that will emerge."[18]

Read Genesis 14:1-16 and fill in the blanks below with the missing details using this word bank:

Dead Sea	Lot	goods
318	twelve	tar pits

After _____ years, the kings of Sodom, Gomorrah, Admah, Zeboiim, and Bela banded together and stopped paying tribute and being subject to King Kedorlaomer (also spelled Chedorlaomer) of Elam. (v. 4)

One year later, King Kedorlaomer (Chedorlaomer) conquered a whole bunch of other territories and then fought the five rebel kings in the valley of the _____ _____. (vv. 5-9)

The valley of the Dead Sea was filled with _____ _____, and some of the fleeing army fell into them while others escaped into the mountains. (v. 10)

The invaders plundered Sodom and Gomorrah and also captured _____, Abram's nephew, carrying off everything he owned. (vv. 11-12)

One of Lot's men escaped and reported everything to Abram, who mobilized _____ men from his household to pursue the victorious army and get Lot back. (vv. 13-14)

Abram won the battle and brought back Lot as well as all the other _____. (vv. 14-16)

What did you learn about Abram's character?

Some of the gals in the pilot study group came up with these insights:

- He was a man of action.
- He was brave.
- He was a warrior.
- He protected what he cared about.
- He never left anyone behind.
- He prepared but trusted.

Abram possessed the qualities of loyalty and bravery, taking on a daunting enemy against the odds. We will learn from the last verses in the chapter where Abram found this kind of courage. He was delivered because He knew his Deliverer.

When Abram battled enemies who had taken a family member captive, he got involved but recognized God Most High's role in helping him. Abram went the distance, traveling 240 miles to make this rescue!

Like Abram, we can assume our position under God's authority and fight against the odds knowing He is on our side. We can do things His way, trusting His instructions and boundaries. Faith is required to trust El Elyon and believe He is stronger than any foe. Or we can try to figure things out our own way, relying on our logic and intellect—and eventually succumb to worry and fear. To put it simply, we can trust in our supreme God or we can try to navigate our lives on our own.

Consider the problems you listed in yesterday's lesson on page 26. In light of El Elyon's ability to deliver Abram, what encouragement or new perspective do you gain in regards to your own present battles?

You may not be fighting on a physical battlefield, but I wonder if sometimes you feel as though your problems outnumber your blessings. Fear, bad habits, a difficult relationship, financial hardship, and so many other issues can feel like real enemies. Other times, our "enemies" are human. Your boss, in-laws, or ex-friends may seem to have more money, position, or power. No matter how high they seem to be sitting, El Elyon is higher. We must be careful not to elevate people above their level as humans made in the image of God. They are not God, and they are not our enemies. Ephesians 6:12 reminds us, "For we are not fighting against flesh-and-blood enemies, but against evil rulers and authorities of the unseen world, against mighty powers in this dark world, and against evil spirits in the heavenly places."

The odds don't tell the final story. Like my daughter's college roommate, we can focus on the size of our God more than the size of our situations. El Elyon is the Deliverer, and we can be delivered because we know Him!

Now let's finish the story where El Elyon ("God Most High") is first mentioned and see a unique foreshadowing of our ultimate Deliverer.

Read Genesis 14:17-24 and answer the following questions:

What roles are used to describe Melchizedek? (v. 18)

What words does Melchizedek use in describing God in his blessing to Abram? (vv. 19-20)

Extra Insight

"Most Jewish commentators concur that Salem is Jerusalem, 'the city of peace.'"[19]

This passage is full of first mentions. We see the first mention of priesthood, tithing, and the name El Elyon! Melchizedek is a mysterious character in that he is both king and priest. We found that Abram responded very differently to the kings of Salem and Sodom. He offered 10 percent to Melchizedek (which foreshadows the tithe for the future priesthood) but refused to take any of the king of Sodom's offer.

Let's look at the contrast we find in these two kings. Star anything on this chart that stands out to you:

King of Salem	King of Sodom
Melchizedek = "king of righteousness"	Bera = "be evil" (14:2)
Salem comes from the root word for peace	Sodom often equated with sin
Abram accepted blessing and gave one-tenth	Abram rejected offer of property

Abram knew God's blessing was coming because He had promised it to him (Genesis 12), and he didn't want anyone to ever associate his future blessings with the city of Sodom. Yet even he could not have appreciated what blessing would come through the priestly line of Melchizedek.

Our supreme God who stands outside of time and space knew even then that He would sacrifice His own Son to restore His relationship with us. Through progressive revelation we know what Abram could not have understood at the time these events occurred. Priests mediate the relationship between God and people. Melchizedek was the first priest, and Jesus is associated with his lineage.

Read the following passages from Hebrews, and then answer the question below:

¹This Melchizedek was king of the city of Salem and also a priest of God Most High. When Abraham was returning home after winning a

great battle against the kings, Melchizedek met him and blessed him.
²Then Abraham took a tenth of all he had captured in battle and gave
it to Melchizedek. The name Melchizedek means "king of justice," and
king of Salem means "king of peace." ³There is no record of his father
or mother or any of his ancestors—no beginning or end to his life. He
remains a priest forever, resembling the Son of God.

(Hebrews 7:1-3)

Extra Insights

Some theologians refer to Melchizedek as a Christ-type in the Old Testament.[20]

¹⁵This change has been made very clear since a different priest, who is
like Melchizedek, has appeared. ¹⁶Jesus became a priest, not by meeting
the physical requirement of belonging to the tribe of Levi, but by the
power of a life that cannot be destroyed. ¹⁷And the psalmist pointed this
out when he prophesied,

> *"You are a priest forever in the order of Melchizedek."*

(Hebrews 7:15-17)

What connection is there between Melchizedek and Christ?

Christ serves as the mediator between God and people according to the priestly order of Melchizedek. God has always been and continues to be in the business of delivering His people. He rescues us with all the power and authority of the Most High God. El Elyon is His name, and Jesus is His Son who mediates a new covenant through the priestly line first mentioned in Genesis 14. God delivered Abram that day in battle, and He longs to deliver you in yours. Through Christ, we have direct access to God Most High.

Behold

Today we have beheld El Elyon, God Most High, who delivered Abram from his enemies and foreshowed the Messiah through the king and priest Melchizedek.

Believe

Write a brief statement of belief:

I believe that El Elyon is supreme over _____
in my life today.

Bloom

We can be delivered because we know the Deliverer. What new perspective can you take today when you think about the obstacles you recorded on page 26?

Like Abram, we can focus on the size of our God more than the size of our problems. Even if the odds don't seem to be in our favor, we can draw near to the God Most High and know that in Christ we have a high priest who is advocating on our behalf.

Talk with God

El Elyon, You are the God Most High. You are Supreme over all creation. You know the battles I'm facing right now. Give me Your eyes to see them, and help me to trust You to get me through. I often find myself trying to figure out the odds in my situation. Instead, help me to focus on Your mighty power and rest in You alone. Amen.

Memory Verse Exercise

Read the Memory Verse on page 12 several times, and then fill in the blanks below as you recite it:

_____ the _____ for the _____ of his _____.
_____ the _____ in the _____ of his _____.
(Psalm 29:2)

Big Idea

We can be delivered because we know the Deliverer, and His name is El Elyon, God Most High.

Day 5: El Roi—The God Who Sees Me

I received the long text and read it slowly. Then I read it again. She accused me of saying things I never said. She assumed stories I had written were about her when they weren't. I sat stunned. She didn't want to meet, talk it out, or work through it. She was ending our friendship completely and asking me to never contact her again.

A cry of injustice rose inside of me. I felt misunderstood. While I wanted to call a friend to "vent," I knew I needed to think, pray, and allow some time to pass before speaking a word that would likely fall in the gossip category. I didn't want to devalue someone made in God's image just because I felt pain.

"Do you see this, God?" I muttered aloud as I sat in my van in the school parking lot waiting for my daughter to come out of her activity. I knew the answer. He did see, and I felt the comfort of His Holy Spirit reminding me of His precious name El Roi, the God who sees me.

We've already learned that El is the generic name for God. We've seen that God is Elohim, the Mighty Creator. We also have seen that He is El Elyon, the God Most High. I love it that we can end this week with an El name that highlights God's personal involvement in our lives. He is transcendent *and* personal. Today we will return to Abram's story to examine the only passage in Scripture where we find the name El Roi.

Scripture Focus

Genesis 16

Begin by reading Genesis 16:1-6 and answer the following questions:

What problem did Sarai have? (v. 1)

What solution did Sarai suggest? (vv. 2-3)

After she was pregnant, how did Hagar begin to treat Sarai? (v. 4)

Who did Sarai blame? (v. 5)

How did Sarai treat Hagar? (v. 6)

Now to our modern ears this may sound very foreign. Yet at the time, it wasn't that uncommon for infertile women to use their servants as surrogates. The child technically would have belonged to Sarai.

While we can't really know what was going on in the hearts and minds of these very real individuals, what are some possible reasons Hagar might have treated Sarai with contempt?

Hagar was an Egyptian slave. Abram and Sarai had been in Egypt because of a famine in the land of Israel (Genesis 12:10). Perhaps she felt her slave position was elevated now that she was carrying the master's child, or maybe it was something else; Hagar began to treat Sarai with contempt. The Hebrew word used here is *qalal* and it means "to be slight, be swift, be trifling, be of little account, be light."[21] Hagar slighted her mistress, Sarai, which may have put salt in the wound of her infertility. Sarai's inability to bear a child could have made her feel inadequate in a culture that equated children with blessing, status, and inheritance.

When we feel slighted or someone presses on the bruises of our lives, our natural reaction often can match Sarai's. First, she blamed someone else, and then she lashed back harshly. The Scriptures say she mistreated Hagar so badly that Hagar ran away. When pain stings in our lives, even if the pain is from our doing, blame and retribution can instinctively rear their ugly heads.

Sarai had set out to fulfill God's promises in a human way. She used her own logic and reason instead of waiting on God to fulfill His promise. In fact, her view of God was that He was the One preventing her from the blessing of a child. Rather than encourage her to wait and trust the Lord, Abram went along with her plans; and their decision had consequences that impacted others, especially Hagar. Their decision started a vicious cycle of contempt and mistreatment that compounded the pain both Hagar and Sarai were experiencing.

Think of a time when you experienced unfair treatment. Whether it was a slight at work or a significant betrayal, record the situation below:

What were your initial thoughts and emotions when you felt mistreated?

I love that God allows us to see the flaws of the biblical characters. Their failures give me hope as I see the Lord using imperfect people when they choose to turn toward Him. I understand Hagar's urge to run away. I have felt it many times. I love that the Lord didn't abandon her, an Egyptian slave, in the desert. At times the focus in Scripture on Abraham's descendants—the nation of Israel—might tempt us to think that God is unfairly partial. Yet here we find that God cared deeply about a foreign slave's mistreatment.

Read Genesis 16:11-16 and summarize the rest of the story in your own words:

What name does Hagar use for the Lord in verse 13?

Hagar discovered that in our lowest moments, someone sees us. He sees our pain. He hears our cries.

Take a moment to read the following verses and circle any key words that stand out to you:

You keep track of all my sorrows.
You have collected all my tears in your bottle.
You have recorded each one in your book.
(Psalm 56:8)

The LORD is watching everywhere,
keeping his eye on both the evil and the good.
(Proverbs 15:3)

How do these verses support Hagar's name for God?

He is the God who sees us. We can rest in the fact that He is never unaware of what we are going through. With the name Elohim, God revealed His character as the mighty Creator. He is the Holy Other who is so far beyond all that we can comprehend. Yet even though He sits outside of time and possesses a transcendence so great, He also is El Roi, the God who sees each one of us.

El Roi saw Hagar, but He didn't promise a quick fix to all her problems. He sees, but He also sees the larger picture outside of the constraints of time. He is omniscient; He knows the role that Hagar's child will play in the future.

Read Genesis 16:8. The angel approached Hagar and asked a question. What was it?

The angel asked where Hagar had come from and where she was going. This question reminds me of God asking Adam and Eve where they were in the garden (Genesis 3:8-9). Remember, God is omnipresent, so He already knew. Similarly, when the Lord spoke to Elijah in the wilderness after he was threatened and

mistreated, He asked him, "What are you doing here?" (1 Kings 19:9). Questions can help us identify how we arrived at our places of discouragement. God isn't gathering information with His questions; He is helping us see our own situations better.

Sometimes I can feel something weighing on me, but I'm not sure exactly what it is. I must take time to reflect and identify what has happened that day, what I'm feeling about it, and how God would have me address it.

Let's take a moment to consider the first part of the angel's question to Hagar and evaluate where we've been lately. Take a quick inventory, answering with one word or phrase to describe where you are:

In your circumstances: What is going on in your life right now?

In your emotions: What word describes your feelings today?

In this season: What is currently your most important task?

I'm coming from just having dropped off three children at college and getting the last one started in high school. Emotionally, I feel drained as I learn to release my children and try not to fix their problems. This past season has been full of mothering, listening, hosting gatherings, and moving into a different home.

Now, let's tackle the second part of the question the angel asked. Where are you headed? What changes do you see ahead?

Sometimes God calls us to have a boundary and walk away from abuse or mistreatment. Other times the boundaries are set for us, and a relationship we want to hold on to is over when we wish it wasn't. In other situations, like Hagar's, God calls us to stay the course. He asks us to go right back into a difficult marriage, work situation, or church conflict with a new perspective, holding on to His promises.

What new perspective is God inviting you to embrace? ?

The next season for me looks like more writing, traveling, and teaching. After a busy mothering season and a move, this next season holds more spending time alone and taking the time to get to know new people. As one of the girls in the pilot study group said, we can get so stuck in the past that we can't see what's ahead. El Roi saw Hagar and helped her to see Him by using questions.

When I have been in a season of betrayal or difficulty, such as the day I received that very long text, I have just wanted God to fix it. Have you ever felt that way? While El Roi sees our mistreatment, we have to trust His instructions since He sees the bigger picture. He sent Hagar right back into her situation, promising her that blessings would come. He heard her cry of distress. While her circumstances may not have changed, her hope factor in the midst of them did.

Behold

Today we have beheld El Roi, the God who sees me. The Creator, the Strong One, the Mighty God who spoke the world into existence, sees me. He sees you too.

Believe

Write a statement of belief:

El Roi sees _____ in my life.

Bloom

How does knowing God's name is El Roi encourage you today?

God sees and hears us. He knows when we cry buckets of tears and aren't even sure why we are sad. He celebrates victory with us when we master a new skill or forgive a difficult person. He sees us on those blah days when we aren't even sure we feel anything. He may not instantly fix every predicament we encounter, but we never need doubt His presence.

Talk with God

El Roi, thank You for seeing me. You know what this day has been like. You know the people who are heavy on my heart. Knowing You are with me brings me encouragement that though there is a huge world of people out there, You know me individually. You see my joys and pains. Bring growth in my life as I behold and believe You more. Amen.

Memory Verse Exercise

Read the Memory Verse on page 12 several times, and then fill in the blanks below as you recite it:

_____ *the* _____ *for* _____ _____ *of* _____ _____.
_____*the* _____ *in* _____ _____ *of* ____ _____.
(Psalm 29:2)

Big Idea

I am never alone because El Roi is the God who sees me.

Weekly Wrap Up

Review the Big Idea for each day, and then write any personal application that comes to mind.

Day 1: Hashem—The Name
Big Idea: Our desire is not to misuse God's name but to worship the One who bears it.

Personal Application:_____

_____

Day 2: Elohim—Creator
Big Idea: Elohim created us, and He only makes good things.

Personal Application:_____

_____

Day 3: Elohim—The Strong One
Big Idea: Elohim is stronger than any problems we face today.

Personal Application:_____

_____

Day 4: El Elyon—God Most High
**Big Idea: We can be delivered because we know the Deliverer, and His
name is El Elyon, God Most High.**

Personal Application:_____

_____

Day 5: El Roi—The God Who Sees Me
Big Idea: I am never alone because El Roi is the God who sees me.

Personal Application:_____

_____

Video Viewer Guide: Week 1

God cares about what you care about because God _____

about _____.

Genesis 1:26-27, 31

We have to zoom out to see that God has a _____ _____.

He delights in the _____ of your life.

Psalm 37:23

Genesis 16:13

Matthew 10:29-31

Week 2

EL (PART 2)

El Shaddai, El Olam, El-Elohe-Israel, El Chay

Memory Verse

Those who live in the shelter of the Most High [El Elyon]
    will find rest in the shadow of the Almighty [El Shaddai].
This I declare about the LORD:
He alone is my refuge, my place of safety;
    he is my God, and I trust him.

(Psalm 91:1-2)

Day 1: El Shaddai—All-Sufficient One

Over twenty years ago I met a friend who taught me how she made a very delicious Greek salad. She didn't measure anything but swirled olive oil, red wine vinegar, fresh-squeezed lemon juice, and salt and pepper over lettuce and red peppers. She mixed it all together with freshly minced garlic and then topped it off with feta cheese. My husband adores this salad, and we began making it when we had company for dinner fairly often. It casually became known as the "Spoelstra salad" at church and social gatherings. Several people over the years have asked us for the recipe after tasting it.

About five years ago we brought the salad to our new small group Bible study only to find someone else there had brought the exact same salad. We called it "our" salad, and she claimed it was "her" salad. After asking where she got the recipe, we found that it could be traced back to me. I had taught the person who taught her. In reality, the salad doesn't belong to either of us. Even my Greek friend didn't make up the recipe; she learned it from her mother who likely learned from hers.

Can you think of something that you claim as your signature "thing" (recipe, style, ability, accomplishment, etc.)? If so, who or what deserves much of the credit for your signature thing?

My small group friend and I still tease about who owns the rights to "the" salad, but ultimately each ingredient can be traced back to a loving God who supplies everything we have. He grew the lettuce. He made the sheep whose milk makes the feta cheese. Humans may press the olives to make the oil, but Elohim, the Mighty Creator, made those olives! While it can seem like people have accomplished so much, none of it is possible without the Mighty Creator we studied last week. He gives us energy, breath, creativity, and resources. We can trace everything back to the source, and the trail ends with God. Today we will find Him revealing more of His character through His name El Shaddai, the All-Sufficient One.

The Hebrew word *shad* means "breast"—specifically a woman's breast.[3] We find the word *shad* in Isaiah 66:10-11:

> "Rejoice with Jerusalem!
>   Be glad with her, all you who love her
>   and all you who mourn for her.

Scripture Focus

Genesis 17:1-8

Extra Insights

El Shaddai is sometimes spelled El Shadday since Strong's Concordance lists the Hebrew word as Shadday.[1]

The meaning of El Shaddai has been the subject of much debate. "Some believe that it speaks of God in His might and power as seen in His judgments."[2] Others lean toward the definition as "All-sufficient One."

Drink deeply of her glory
   even as an infant drinks at its mother's comforting breasts."

What words would you use to describe the relationship between a mother and her nursing child?

When I breastfed my children, I knew how dependent they were on me. I also knew I could quiet them when they were fussy by feeding them. I was their sole source of nourishment. This is a picture of El Shaddai. His name reveals God as the pourer of life, nourishment, and blessings. While the Hebrew word is associated with nourishment, I also want us to consider the English translation "all-sufficient." Merriam-Webster defines *sufficient* as "enough to meet the needs of a situation or a proposed end."[4] When we say that El Shaddai is the all-sufficient One, we are believing that He is enough for us.

Take a moment to reflect on the truth that God is enough. In what ways do you have enough today because of the provision of El Shaddai?

We have enough food, time, people, and possessions. It may not always feel like it, but our God has promised to supply all of our needs (Philippians 4:19). Here is the truth we want to explore today: W*hen we recognize God's sufficiency, we can pursue greater dependency.* Today we will return to the story of Abram and Sarai for the first mention of El Shaddai in Scripture. Here are a few quick reminders to give us context as we jump back into Genesis:

- God promised Abram and Sarai a child and a multitude of descendants when Abram was seventy-five years old.
- After over ten years of waiting, Sarai gave her Egyptian slave Hagar to sleep with Abram in the hope of having a child through her. (Abram was eighty-six at this time.)
- When Hagar gave birth to a son named Ishmael, it caused enmity between her and Sarai.
- Hagar ran away, but God revealed Himself as El Roi, the God who sees, and she returned to Abram and Sarai.

Let's pick up the story after Abram and Sarai have tried to force God's promise to fulfillment using their own logic and means.

Read Genesis 17:1-2 and fill in the following chart:

Abram's age (v. 1)	
God's revealed name (v. 1)	
God's instructions to Abram (v. 1)	
The covenant promise given (v. 2)	

God had promised Abram twenty-four years earlier that he would have many descendants. He now was well advanced in age, and he and his wife had grown impatient with God's promises. They used human logic to try to help God along. I have done it too. From their example we learn that we can't try to force the fulfillment of God's promises on our timetable.

What I love about El Shaddai, our All-Sufficient One, is that He enters the scene after Abram and Sarai have tried to force fulfillment. By using Hagar as a surrogate, they created a power struggle that would continue. While our decisions certainly have consequences, El Shaddai understands our weakness and doesn't kick us to the curb when we do not wait on Him and take matters into our own hands. After we make a mess of things, God can still fulfill His promises to us.

Read Genesis 17:3-8 and answer the following questions:

How did Abram respond after El Shaddai appeared to him? (v. 3)

What did God change in Abram's life? (v. 5)

What blessings did El Shaddai confirm would come to Abraham? (vv. 4, 6-8)

When Abram and Sarai recognized their own insufficiency, it drew them to bow down and yield to God. It drew them nearer to Him. Can you relate personally to them as they recognized their insufficiency and their need for dependency on El Shaddai?

Reflect on any past or current situations where you have tried to fix things your own way and then realized your need to stop working,

cling to God, and wait for His timing. If something comes to mind, record it below:

Abram had tried things his own way, but then he fell on his face before the Lord. He didn't justify himself. He didn't shame God for taking too long. He got low. This was a sign of deep respect and dependency. After Abram took this posture, God began to speak. He reaffirmed His covenant and gave Abram a new name. Abram means "exalted father,"[5] but Abraham means "father of a multitude."[6] Every time someone spoke his name, he was to be reminded that God had plans for his children, grandchildren, and a multitude of descendants.

God promised Abraham not just an heir but a nation that would include kings and a kingdom. Abraham couldn't out-sin God's grace, and neither can we. Just because you may have tried to "help" God out and may have made a mess of things in the past, God isn't done with you. Abram and Sarai made mistakes along the way. You and I have too. The enemy wants to convince us that God's plan for us is beyond fixing. It isn't true. God is our supplier. If we are still alive, then our story isn't fully written. We can start today by leaning into God. This means that, like Abram, we get low. God's sufficiency calls us to pursue greater dependency.

What might it look like for you to "get low" in response to El Shaddai today, taking a posture of deep respect and dependency? Take a moment to ask the Lord to reveal anything to you, and record it below:

Abram fell down on the ground in weakness but rose up as Abraham, the father of multitudes. God calls us to stop striving in our own strength so we can seek His.

Behold

Today we have beheld the name God revealed to Abram: El Shaddai, the All-Sufficient One.

Believe

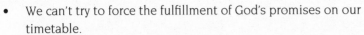

Based on what we learned through Abram's transformation into Abraham in Genesis 17, these three truths stick out to me:

- We can't try to force the fulfillment of God's promises on our timetable.
- After we make a mess of things, God can still fulfill His promises to us when we choose to get low.
- When we recognize God's sufficiency, we can pursue greater dependency.

Place a star next to one of these three statements above as the one that most resonates with you, or write your own statement of belief in El Shaddai:

_____

_____

_____

Bloom

After El Shaddai appeared to Abram, He commanded him to serve faithfully and pursue a blameless life (Genesis 17:1). God works to redeem our messes, but He instructs us to avoid them as well. El Shaddai calls us to serve Him faithfully and seek to live in step with His instructions. With Him as the supplier of nourishment and life, it takes the pressure off. Mothers don't expect their newborns to walk, but they do encourage them to eat what is provided for them.

What would it look like today for you to lean into El Shaddai and trust Him as your All-Sufficient One? Briefly describe how your life might look different as you grow in belief that El Shaddai is sufficient to fulfill every promise He has made to you:

We found today that Abraham's faith wasn't fully mature. Ours isn't either. We are pursuing imperfect progress—growth in believing God more as we behold and believe Him. Then, as we behold and believe, He gives us the power to bloom in greater faithfulness and purity.

Talk with God

El Shaddai, You are all that I need. Help me to see clearly that You are the sufficiency in my life. I believe that You are enough. When I am tempted toward self-sufficiency, help me to get low and receive from You. Thank You for revealing Your name as El Shaddai to free me from fear and worry. Amen.

Memory Verse Exercise

Big Idea

When we recognize El Shaddai's sufficiency, we can pursue greater dependency.

Read the Memory Verse on page 42 several times, and then fill in the blanks below as you recite it:

Those who live in the _____ of the Most High [El Elyon]
 will find rest in the _____ of the Almighty [El Shaddai].
This I declare about the LORD:
He alone is my _____, my place of safety;
 he is my God, and I trust him.

(Psalm 91:1-2)

Day 2: El Shaddai—Promise Keeper

Scripture Focus

Genesis 35; Job 40:1-5

When my husband and I were dating, he promised that he would always be strong enough to pick me up. After twenty-four years of marriage, I love to remind him of his silly promise. We made other promises on our wedding day, however, that are no laughing matter. We promised to be faithful to each other. After his parents' divorce during his teen years, my husband personally felt the weight of broken promises. Soon after our marriage, we decided to never even joke about breaking our covenant vows.

The wounds of unfulfilled promises can leave us feeling betrayed and vulnerable. It can become difficult to trust others when those we expected to keep their promises didn't.

Can you think of some promises made to you that weren't kept?
Record one or two below:

Perhaps a work contract, friendship, or marriage has ended in your life due to promises broken. God doesn't gloss over what you've been through. He knows betrayal firsthand. The people He loved cheated on Him with other gods. They murdered His prophets and crucified His Son. Yet in the midst of it all, He remains a promise keeper. Today we will continue our study of El Shaddai, looking at its multifaceted meaning. El Shaddai is our All-Sufficient One, but His name also hints at His character as a Promise Keeper. One author has said, "Until the time of Moses, when another divine name was revealed, the patriarchs considered El *Shadday* as the covenant name of God."[7] Covenants differ from contracts. They reveal the relationship between God and people. People can also enter into covenants with other people. In a covenant, both parties agree to certain conditions and advantages.[8] God made covenants with Noah, Abraham, Moses, and David, and He ushered in a New Covenant through Christ.

The covenant God made with Abraham is referred to as the Abrahamic Covenant. Yesterday we learned about those promises. What are some of the things God said would be in Abraham's future? (Look back at Genesis 12 or 17 if you can't remember.)

El Shaddai appeared to Abraham and told him about descendants, nations, kings, and land that He would pour out on future generations. He said the whole world would be blessed through Abraham. However, these promises were much like the one about having a son. There was a gap between promise and fulfillment.

Patience is a tough one for me. I prefer things to move fast rather than slow. I walk fast. I talk fast. When someone is taking too long to turn on the TV, I have an inner dialogue to keep from grabbing the remote. God may not have promised us descendants like Abraham, but He has promised us many things:

- He tells us we don't need to worry because He will take care of us (Matthew 6:25).
- He has promised us that Jesus will return (John 14:2, 28).
- He says He will never leave or forsake us (Hebrews 13:5).

These are just a few of the hundreds of promises we can claim from Scripture. The challenge comes when there is a time gap between the promise and fulfillment. Abraham was well acquainted with that time gap, and so am I. God has promised that He is always with me, but sometimes I don't feel His presence. He has promised me He will provide for my needs, but when an unexpected medical bill or car repair throws off my budget, my doubts kick into high gear. Are you experiencing one of those gaps between promise and fulfillment right now?

The gals in the pilot study group and I discussed micro and macro waiting. Life can be full of micro waiting. We wait for the computer to boot up or the dryer to finish. Macro waiting revolves around more significant situations where we need patience, such as waiting on healing, a desired relationship, or a job.

Take a moment to identify both a micro and macro waiting example in your life:

Micro:

Macro:

It's OK if you don't have anything big going on right now in the patience department. Just wait! A macro wait might be just around the corner, and we can be prepared as we learn from the biblical narrative.

Abram and Sarai grew discouraged in waiting. Have you ever felt that way?

What are some general tendencies people have when they are impatient?

Those who are impatient to get married might make a hasty decision. If we are impatient in traffic, we might cause an accident. When we are impatient with God, we might start to think He won't keep His promise or needs our help. Today we are going to look at Jacob's and Job's interactions with El Shaddai in Scripture to see a broader perspective of God's nature as a promise keeper.

Abraham and Sarah did have a son, and they named him Isaac. Isaac had twin boys named Jacob and Esau, and Jacob encountered El Shaddai much like his grandfather Abraham had.

Read Genesis 35:1-15 and place the events below in the order they appear in the text, numbering them 1–6:

_____ A. Jacob built an altar in Luz.

_____ B. God changed Jacob's name to Israel.

_____ C. God revealed Himself as El Shaddai, God Almighty, and commanded Jacob to be fruitful and multiply.

_____ D. Jacob told everyone in his household to get rid of pagan idols, purify themselves, and put on clean clothing.

_____ E. God told Jacob to move to Bethel and build an altar there.

_____ F. Jacob set up a stone pillar to mark the place where God had spoken to Him.

Go back and reread Genesis 35:11-12 again, and write below any references to the original covenant God made with Abraham:

Extra Insight

This encounter in Genesis 35 wasn't Jacob's first visit to Bethel. Bethel was where Jacob wrestled with God (Genesis 32:24-32).

Two generations had passed, and now the promises were coming to fruition regarding the land. Even though Abraham didn't see the entire fulfillment of the promises God made to Him, he believed them by faith. The writer of Hebrews sums up this story succinctly.

Read Hebrews 11:8-16 below, and circle every occurrence of the words *promise* and *promised*:

⁸*It was by faith that Abraham obeyed when God called him to leave home and go to another land that God would give him as his inheritance. He went without knowing where he was going.* ⁹*And even when he reached the land God promised him, he lived there by faith— for he was like a foreigner, living in tents. And so did Isaac and Jacob, who inherited the same promise.* ¹⁰*Abraham was confidently looking forward to a city with eternal foundations, a city designed and built by God.*

¹¹*It was by faith that even Sarah was able to have a child, though she was barren and was too old. She believed that God would keep his promise.* ¹²*And so a whole nation came from this one man who was as good as dead—a nation with so many people that, like the stars in the sky and the sand on the seashore, there is no way to count them.*

¹³*All these people died still believing what God had promised them. They did not receive what was promised, but they saw it all from a distance and welcomed it. They agreed that they were foreigners and nomads here on earth.* ¹⁴*Obviously people who say such things are looking forward to a country they can call their own.* ¹⁵*If they had longed for the*

country they came from, they could have gone back. ¹⁶*But they were looking for a better place, a heavenly homeland. That is why God is not ashamed to be called their God, for he has prepared a city for them.*

As we seek to understand El Shaddai as the Mighty God who is a promise keeper, what stands out to you after reading this passage?

The writer of Hebrews mentions that these people saw themselves as foreigners and nomads here on earth. I have a tendency to settle in and forget that this is a temporary home. Having the mind-set of a foreigner or nomad impacts our view of life and circumstances. It lends perspective to the suffering in this life. Job was a man who knew about perspective change firsthand. He used the name El Shaddai more than anyone else in the Bible. Of the forty-eight mentions of El Shaddai, we find thirty-one of them in Job.⁹ God's plan puzzled Job, who wrestled with suffering and difficulty. As a result, he had many questions for El Shaddai.

Are there some answers you would like from El Shaddai right now? Knowing that He is an Almighty promise keeper, what questions would you like to ask Him about the gap between His promises and what you see around you?

I would like to ask God why the innocent suffer, why life is so hard, and why He doesn't send Jesus to return . . . today. God invites us to ask, but we must be prepared for the answers of El Shaddai, the Almighty God. He answered Job's questions with a few of His own, including: "Where were you when I laid the foundations of the earth?" (Job 38:4) and "Have you ever commanded the morning to appear and caused the dawn to rise in the east?" (Job 38:12).

God welcomes our honest questions, but may we never lose our sense of awe for who God is. My pastor recently preached about Job, and he asked each person listening to consider how well we are doing at running our own lives. He wondered how many of us handle our time, money, and health so well that we should be put in charge of running the entire planet. He jokingly asked how many of us could grow our own food if we tried. (I found that hitting close to home as I have no green in my thumb whatsoever!) Yet sometimes we think we

know better than God about how things should go. I'm so guilty of thinking I know a better way. If we aren't careful, we can become God's critic without even realizing it.

After asking seventy-seven questions of Job, El Shaddai had one final question:

¹Then the LORD said to Job,

²"Do you still want to argue with the Almighty? [El Shaddai]
    You are God's critic, but do you have the answers?"
³Then Job replied to the LORD,

⁴"I am nothing—how could I ever find the answers?
    I will cover my mouth with my hand.
⁵I have said too much already.
    I have nothing more to say."

(Job 40:1-5)

El Shaddai can be tender like a nursing mother, providing all that we need, but He also is the Almighty maker of heaven and earth.

As you sit in awe of the Almighty, how does the response of Job resonate with you? Write your own prayer of response as if El Shaddai has addressed you like Job, saying, "You are God's critic, but do you have all the answers?"

We can trust the One who has kept every promise He has made. After sin separated us from Him, He sent His one and only Son as a sacrifice for us. El Shaddai fulfilled the plan He had all along to redeem us. He is the One who has all the answers.

Behold

Today we have beheld El Shaddai as an Almighty God who keeps His promises.

Believe

Write a statement of belief, filling in the blank in a specific or general way (there is no right answer here):

El Shaddai keeps His promises so I know He will _____

_____ in my life.

Bloom

We can learn to patiently wait for God to accomplish His plans. He may fulfill a promise in our lives tomorrow, or it may not happen until we reach heaven. While this may be difficult to accept, it is our choice either to lean into our faith or to lean away from it. We can learn from Abraham, Jacob, and Job to live by faith even if we only see from a distance. People in our lives may not have kept their promises to us, but El Shaddai will never betray us. Everything He has said, He will do.

Talk with God

El Shaddai, You are the Almighty Promise Keeper. Give me patience in the gap between Your promises and their fulfillment in my life. Open my heart to believe Your promises over my own circumstances and feelings. You will do everything You have said. Give me diligence to study Your promises and faith to believe them as they relate to my life. Amen.

Memory Verse Exercise

Big Idea

We can wait patiently knowing that El Shaddai will fulfill every promise He has made.

Read the Memory Verse on page 42 several times, and then fill in the blanks below as you recite it:

¹*Those who live in the _____ of the Most _____ [El Elyon]*

will find rest in the _____ of the _____

[El Shaddai].

²*This I declare about the LORD:*

He alone is my _____, my place of _____;

he is my God, and I _____ him.

(Psalm 91:1-2)

Day 3: El Olam—Everlasting God

Scripture Focus

Genesis 21

Throughout the years of attending Bible studies, I've seen women use many ideas for sharing prayer requests and praying for one another. One leader gave each attendee an index card and asked us to write down one prayer request. She told us we would exchange with another woman at the end of the group to pray in pairs. Sounds easy. Write down a prayer request. On that particular day, my mind and heart felt so jumbled. Have you ever had days when you weren't even sure how to ask someone to pray for you? Here is a question that helps me when I find myself in this predicament: "What is getting my attention lately?"

My thought life can be all over the place, but this question helps me evaluate what has been on my mind. Some attention-getters for me today include:

- conversations with my college kids about struggles with relationships, schoolwork, and so on;
- feeling time pressure to get things done;
- juggling when my daughter needs rides, who I'm meeting with, when things are due, my next travel date, and so on.

I might have a whole different list next week, but these things have been getting my attention lately. My mind too often seems to be occupied with the next thing on my schedule. In fact, if someone collected every prayer request index card I've ever written at a Bible study, I'd guess at least half of them are somehow related to time management.

Take a moment and write down a few bullet points of things that are getting your attention lately:

-

-

-

You may be in a season when you have a lot of time on your hands. Maybe you're a stay-at-home mom and your kids are in school during the daytime. Perhaps you are retired and find you have some margin in your calendar. Or you may feel as though you are running the race of life. You have work, family, volunteering or ministry, and appointments, and you feel the impact of others' needs affecting yours.

With social media, online games, and phones at our fingertips, it often seems there are greater temptations to waste time today. With the ability to scroll through others' lives, I find new sources of guilt. I see others using their time for date nights to value their marriages. I should be doing that. People are taking their children on individual trips and making special memories. Add that to my list. Someone just posted their predawn run and a picture of the beautiful sky. Ugh. I should definitely be exercising more. There never seems to be enough hours in the day to do it all.

Yet in the midst of our struggle with time, we serve a God who stands outside of time. He created time and knows all about our online calendars and personal planners. His name is El Olam, the Everlasting God. He is the God of the Ages, and His name is often translated "Eternal" or "Everlasting" in our English Bibles.

The first mention of El Olam in the Bible is found in an encounter with Abraham. Yesterday we talked about his grandson Jacob; today we will back up a bit in the biblical narrative to Abraham's experience with El Olam.

Read Genesis 21:1-7 and write below what Sarah says God has brought her. If your Bible has a study note, find the meaning of Isaac's name or look it up online.

Extra Insights

Abimelech noted that God was with Abraham, helping him in all he did. Certainly he recognized the miracle of Abraham and Sarah having a child long past the years of childbearing, and he had personally experienced a healing when Abraham prayed for him (Genesis 20:17).

Tamarisk trees live a long time and consist of hard wood and evergreen leaves. "This tree was a type of the ever-enduring grace of the faithful, covenant-keeping God."[10]

God brought this elderly couple laughter with the birth of the son God had promised them long ago. However, not every promise God made through the Abrahamic covenant was fulfilled in Isaac. Like Abraham, we celebrate promises fulfilled and keep looking forward to those that remain unfulfilled. We will see that God works over time, revealing more of Himself to each generation in the Genesis account.

At this time, Abraham's family was living in the land of King Abimelech in the country of the Philistines. It is here that we find the first mention of El Olam.

Read Genesis 21:22-34 and answer the following questions:

What did Abimelech say was evident in Abraham's life? (v. 22)

What was Abraham's complaint to Abimelech? (v. 25)

What did Abraham name the place where they made a treaty? (v. 31)

What was the meaning of the name? (v. 31)

What did Abraham plant there? (v. 33)

Whom does your translation say Abraham worshiped there? (v. 33)

Abraham discovered that his God was El Olam, the eternal God. One source observes that "the word 'Olam,' which is rendered 'everlasting,' contains in itself both the idea of a 'secret,' and also of 'time,' or of 'an age.'"[11] Olam is a word used throughout the Bible, but it is only paired with El a handful of times where God reveals His character as the God of the Ages.

Abraham worshiped El Olam, God of the Ages, knowing that some things he could see in his present age and others he wouldn't see until later. God gave him a child in his old age, but God also had promised him the land of Canaan. Yet the final verse in this chapter says that Abraham stayed with the Philistines for a long time. He saw fulfillment of some of God's promises but was still waiting from a distance to see others come to fruition.

We live in this same place of already and not yet. We have seen God fulfill many of His promises to us, but in other areas we are still waiting. Like Abraham, we can learn to trust El Olam, the God of the Ages. He transcends time yet chooses to grow our faith over time as we learn to trust Him more and more.

In El Olam we find a God who works throughout the ages. As you reflect on your own personal spiritual history, how have you seen God reveal Himself over time?

Perhaps God has helped you turn from a habitual sin or has comforted you in times of trouble. Maybe you see stages of growth during difficult seasons while other growth comes through greater consistency in your spiritual habits. Sometimes I want to rush growth or answers to prayer. As I understand God as El Olam, I'm reminded that my life is in His hands. I can surrender my time lines when I remember that He is the God of every age.

El Olam is eternal. His timing may not be ours, but we can worship Him as Abraham did, knowing that some things are revealed now and others are still secret. We can surrender our calendar to God, asking Him to show us the best use of our weeks, days, hours, and minutes.

Write a short prayer of faith below regarding the use of your time in the coming week:

Let's end today with a quick look at other places in the Bible where we find God revealing Himself as El Olam. Underline any words related to God's character as eternal, everlasting, and so forth:

Trust in the LORD always,
    for the LORD GOD is the eternal Rock.
(Isaiah 26:4)

Have you never heard?
    Have you never understood?
The LORD is the everlasting God,
    the Creator of all the earth.
He never grows weak or weary.
    No one can measure the depths of his understanding.
(Isaiah 40:28)

But the LORD is the only true God.
    He is the living God and the everlasting King!
The whole earth trembles at his anger.
    The nations cannot stand up to his wrath.
(Jeremiah 10:10)

Praise the LORD, the God of Israel,
    who lives from everlasting to everlasting.
Amen and amen!
(Psalm 41:13)

[1]Lord, you have been our dwelling place
    throughout all generations.
[2]Before the mountains were born
    or you brought forth the whole world,
    from everlasting to everlasting you are God.
(Psalm 90:1-2 NIV)

Through progressive revelation in Scripture we develop a deeper understanding of God so we can know Him more. In a similar way, over the ages of our lives we grow in our relationship with God as we wisely use our time to pursue a relationship with Him.

Behold

Our God is El Olam, who reigns from everlasting to everlasting.

Believe

Write a statement of belief:

El Olam, I believe that You are _____.

Bloom

God's everlasting character helps us find perspective in a culture obsessed with time. How do the truths revealed about God's character as El Olam impact your thinking when it comes to your relationship with the clock and calendar?

While we can struggle to manage our time each day, our God, El Olam, stands outside of time. As we get to know Him more, we can yield to His eternal plan when it comes to what we can see and what we are still believing by faith.

Talk with God

El Olam, You are the Everlasting God. I can't even wrap my mind around what it means that You stand outside of time. So much of my life revolves around schedules. Help me to see You clearly and to focus today on eternal things rather than temporal ones. I worship You as a God who is bigger than my mind can even comprehend! Amen.

Memory Verse Exercise

Read the Memory Verse on page 42 several times, and then fill in the blanks below as you recite it:

¹_____ who live in the _____ of the Most _____
[El Elyon]
    will find _____ in the _____ of the _____
    [El Shaddai].
²This I _____ about the LORD:
    He _____ is my _____, my place of _____;
    he is my _____, and I _____ him.

(Psalm 91:1-2)

Read the Memory Verse on page 42

Big Idea

We live within the framework of time and look to El Olam to help us manage it wisely.

Day 4: El-Elohe-Israel—The God of Me

I recently returned from a trip to celebrate my aunt's seventieth birthday. My sister, mom, cousins, and aunts traveled from all over the country to spend a few days together. We laughed, made memories, and talked about all sorts of subjects. We slept late, took day trips, and ate—and then ate some more.

Scripture Focus

Genesis 32:22-32; 33:18-20

Occasionally we spoke about God. Someone told a story of God's provision. Another shared openly how she was struggling with her faith. I enjoyed our conversations, especially when we talked about our Savior.

On the way home I realized that while we had talked a lot about God, I hadn't spent very much time with Him. During all the busyness of the vacation, I had discussed God but had not personally interacted with Him much. There's a difference between talking about someone and personally spending time with that person. As we discover the character of God as Elohim, El Elyon, or El Shaddai, we don't want to just learn the facts *about* Him. He reveals Himself to us so that we can draw near to Him.

Today we return to the story of Jacob, who had a twin brother named Esau. With the help of his mother, Rebekah, Jacob stole the blessing and the birthright from his firstborn brother. Esau was enraged by this scandal, and Jacob ran away to another town to preserve his life. Jacob found some of his mother's relatives and married two sisters named Leah and Rachel. Their father was Jacob's uncle Laban.

When God increased Jacob's wealth, Laban was often eager to get his hands on it. Eventually Jacob took his wives and left. On the way to the land God had promised through his grandfather Abraham, Jacob knew he would have to pass through his brother Esau's lands. He sent many gifts ahead of him to try to appease the brother whose birthright he had stolen. Then Jacob had an encounter with God.

Read Genesis 32:22-32 and either sketch the scenes or describe them in words in the ovals below:

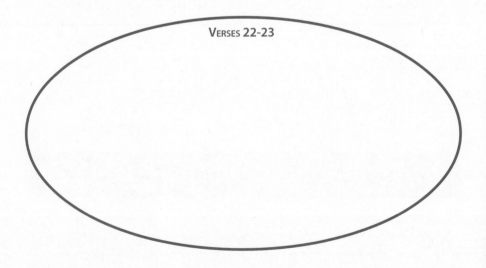

Verses 22-23

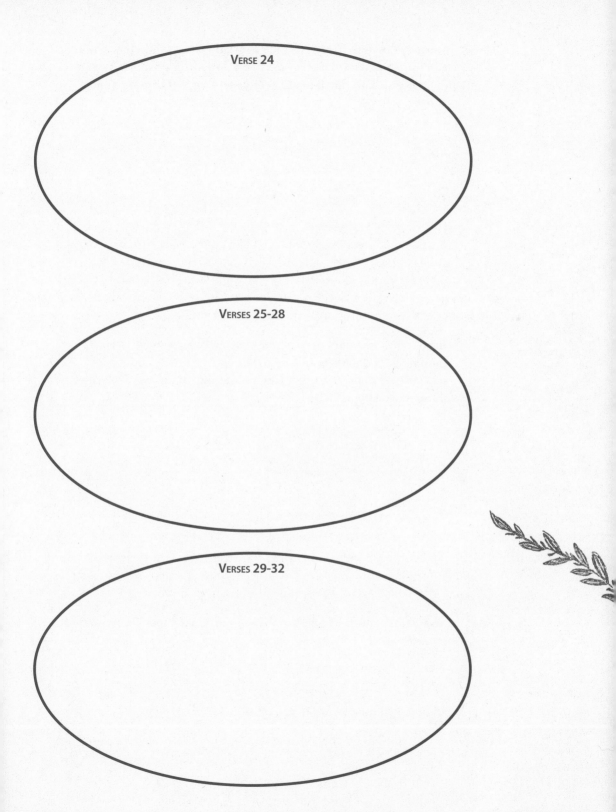

VERSE 24

VERSES 25-28

VERSES 29-32

You may not have been wrestling with God physically in the form of a person, but have you been wrestling through any aspects in your relationship with Him lately? Record anything that comes to mind below:

I find that studying Scripture and dealing with life's disappointments bring me into frequent wrestling matches with the Lord. I ask questions in my journal, seek counsel from others, and resign myself to some elements of mystery when it comes to understanding God. However, when I have truly wrestled through my doubts, I usually find myself coming out closer to God on the other side. I may not have all of my questions answered, but my faith grows as I wrestle.

Have you ever experienced a time of growth as you have wrestled through your doubts or questions? If so, write briefly about any specific questions, circumstances, or seasons where your faith grew through wrestling.

¹⁸*Later, having traveled all the way from Paddan-aram, Jacob arrived safely at the town of Shechem, in the land of Canaan. There he set up camp outside the town. ¹⁹Jacob bought the plot of land where he camped from the family of Hamor, the father of Shechem, for 100 pieces of silver. ²⁰And there he built an altar and named it El-Elohe-Israel.*
(Genesis 33:18-20)

Jacob wrestled with God, seeing Him face to face. In Genesis 33, after his initial meeting with Esau went well, Jacob built an altar. He gathered wood, built a fire, killed an animal, and offered a sacrifice in worship.

Now Read Genesis 33:18-20 in the margin. What name did Jacob give to the altar?

What land did Jacob arrive in that day?

What names do you recognize in the name of the altar, and what do they mean?

Canaan, where Jacob set up camp, was the land that God had promised to give to Abraham's descendants. There he built an altar and named it El-Elohe-Israel. *El* is the word for God, and Israel is the name that Jacob received after his wrestling match with God at Peniel (Genesis 32). This name tells us something about the special relationship between Jacob and his God. Genesis 33:20 is the only verse in the Bible that mentions El-Elohe-Israel.[13]

When Jacob built an altar for the first time in the Promised Land, he dedicated it to the God of Israel. I've heard the phrase "God of Israel" many times, but when studying this passage it struck me that, in this one and only mention of this name in Scripture, it was Israel himself (Jacob) who said it. He basically said, "I will worship the God of me." It would be like me writing a worship song or prayer addressed to the "God of Melissa." Take that in for a moment. That's how personal God (El) was to Jacob.

Yes, God is Elohim, the Mighty Creator. Yes, He is El Roi, the God who sees me. Yes, He is El Shaddai, the All-Sufficient One. We could continue to list so many of His names. Yet we cannot forget that even though He is mighty and set apart as Holy, He wants to be God of our lives, *personally.*

I had the awesome privilege of learning about God from the time I was a little girl. I heard stories about Him at church. I attended camps where His Word was taught. Still, He often felt like this force that was far away from my life of picking out clothes, trying to get schoolwork done, and wondering if people liked me. Though I've come to experience God in a personal way, sometimes distance can creep back into my relationship with God if I'm not careful.

What about you? Have you ever noticed a gap between what you read and know about God and the things on your to-do list—the stuff of everyday life? Where is God in the midst of dentist checkups, dishwasher loading, email answering, and in-law visits? I still need constant realignment to remember that He longs to be the God of Melissa. He cares about my to-do list. Scripture tells us that He delights in the details of our lives (Psalm 37:23). I tend to think about Him more when I'm on the mountaintop of celebration or in the valley of difficulty, but He longs to be our God in the mundane as well. As we study His names, we want to remember that this same God that is omnipotent, omniscient, and omnipresent desires deep relationship with us.

Read the verses on the following page and put a star by the one that most resonates with you today:

[11]"**This command I am giving you today is not too difficult for you, and it is not beyond your reach.** [12]**It is not kept in heaven, so distant that you must ask, 'Who will go up to heaven and bring it down so we can hear it and obey?'** [13]**It is not kept beyond the sea, so far away that you must ask, 'Who will cross the sea to bring it to us so we can hear it and obey?'** [14]**No, the message is very close at hand; it is on your lips and in your heart so that you can obey it.''**

(Deuteronomy 30:11-14)

But as for me, how good it is to be near God!
   I have made the Sovereign LORD my shelter,
   and I will tell everyone about the wonderful things you do.

(Psalm 73:28)

The LORD is near to all who call upon Him,
To all who call upon Him in truth.

(Psalm 145:18 NASB)

"From one man he created all the nations throughout the whole earth. He decided beforehand when they should rise and fall, and he determined their boundaries.

"His purpose was for the nations to seek after God and perhaps feel their way toward him and find him—though he is not far from any one of us. For in him we live and move and exist."

(Acts 17:26-28a)

Come close to God, and God will come close to you. Wash your hands, you sinners; purify your hearts, for your loyalty is divided between God and the world.

(James 4:8)

As God reveals Himself to us through His names, we can revere Him because He is awesome. We also can celebrate that this amazing God wants to be our God. Jacob named an altar, declaring that El-Elohe-Israel reigned in his life. After he wrestled with God, Jacob worshiped Him.

We no longer need to stack wood, kill animals, and light fires to bring offerings to the Lord. Hebrews 10:1 tells us, "The old system under the law of Moses was only a shadow, a dim preview of the good things to come, not the good things themselves. The sacrifices under that system were repeated again and again, year after year, but they were never able to provide perfect cleansing for those who came to worship."

If we no longer need to build an altar and kill an animal, how are we to worship God? Is worship more than what happens at church? When I have wrestled through my circumstances and come out on the other side with an awareness that God is El-Elohe-Melissa, how can I respond?

Read Romans 12:1-2 below and record any insights you receive regarding how you can respond to God after wrestling through your circumstances:

[1]And so, dear brothers and sisters, I plead with you to give your bodies to God because of all he has done for you. Let them be a living and holy sacrifice—the kind he will find acceptable. This is truly the way to worship him. [2]Don't copy the behavior and customs of this world, but let God transform you into a new person by changing the way you think. Then you will learn to know God's will for you, which is good and pleasing and perfect.

(Romans 12:1-2)

We don't put an animal on the altar; we put ourselves up there! This verse highlights God's transforming work in us as we yield ourselves to Him.

You can worship God and ask Him to be "El-Elohe-(your name)," the God of you. You may wrestle with Him. At times you may struggle to bridge the gap between His awesomeness and your mundane routines. Other times you may cry out in your troubles when you can't sense His presence at all. Jacob's altar encourages me that the God of Israel is also the God of me and the God of you. Jacob used the new name God gave to him on the other side of his wrestling with God. Jacob means "deceiver" but Israel means "God contends."[14] Jacob used his transformed name rather than his old one. Through Jesus, we too can be transformed. He has opened the door for us to draw near to God with boldness. We can go right into the presence of God without a guilty conscience because we have been washed by the final blood sacrifice.

Behold

Today we beheld Jacob whose name was changed to Israel and who called out to El-Elohe-Israel.

Believe

Write your name in the blank below:

God, You are El-Elohe- _____ **. You are the God of Me.**

Bloom

When we behold and believe that God is our God, it fills us with wonder and love. God sent His Son so that we could come before Him boldly. The verses we read from Hebrews remind me that the fruit in my life should not be shame. By His blood, Jesus has washed my guilty conscience, and He wants to have first place in my life.

Let's end today listening to any promptings of God in response to our study of Jacob's altar. Take a moment to be still in His presence. Ask questions. Express doubts. Realign beliefs. Do some wrestling if you need to. Write your thoughts, questions, or prayer below:

Beholding the God of Me transforms me to live His way over mine, knowing that my life is in His hands. Today I am yielding to Him. My time, money, thoughts, words, and actions are under His authority.

Talk with God

El-Elohe-Israel, I love that Jacob penned this name for You with His transformed name of Israel. You are the God of me—the transformed me who lives in Christ. You have given me a new identity through Your Son. Help me to draw near to You with boldness, recognizing that while You are the incredibly mighty God of the universe, You are also the God of me. Amen.

Memory Verse Exercise

Read the Memory Verse on page 42 several times, and then fill in the blanks below as you recite it:

¹ _____ *who live in the* _____ *of the* _____ _____
[El Elyon]
   will _____ _____ *in the* _____ *of the*
   _____ **[El Shaddai].**
²*This I* _____ *about the* _____:
   He _____ *is my* _____, *my* _____ *of* _____;
   _____ *is my* _____, *and I* _____ _____.

(Psalm 91:1-2)

Big Idea

The Mighty God of the Universe is also the God of me.

Day 5: El Chay—Living God

Pastor Tony Evans wrote a book about God's names, and in it he tells about a little bird that began to freeze as it tried to fly south for the winter. It eventually fell down when it just couldn't go on anymore. The little bird landed in a pile of manure in a field filled with cows. The situation stunk in more ways than one. Then the bird realized the cow patty was providing warmth and thawing him out. He got so excited he began to sing. A cat heard his song and dug him out and ate him.[15]

Scripture Focus

Joshua 3; Hosea 1:10; Psalm 42:2

We can chuckle at this story, but it reminds me of the tension we feel at times. Often we struggle to fly through life. The world can be a cold and difficult place. When we fall, we wonder if God knows we are stuck in a pile of poopy circumstances. The situations we view as terrible are sometimes the very things God can use to save us. Tony Evans made these applications to the story as well: "First, not everybody who drops manure on you is your enemy. Second, not everybody who digs you out is your friend."[16]

The world can be like that cat. It offers to dig us out of what feels like a crappy situation and makes us feel alive again with sinful pursuits that seem like a rescue in the moment. The lure of the world can tempt us to fill the ache inside with things that seem shiny and exciting.

What are some things that make you feel alive? (They can be things that are good for your soul, or temptations that aren't good for you.)

I feel alive when I'm doing what God created me to do. When I study and write and speak, I feel God's presence. But I will tell you that most times I don't feel like doing those things. I have to discipline myself to sit down and get started—every single time. I'd rather scroll through social media, watch Netflix, answer emails, or organize a closet than sit down and do the things that make me feel alive. Why is that? Can you relate, or are you the opposite?

The Living God sees a bigger picture than we do. He offers us life—abundant life (John 10:10)—and He calls us to push past the path of least resistance. The things we think will give us life, or at least make us feel good in the moment, usually don't give lasting fullness. I've never finished a television marathon or an hour of social media scrolling or an overindulgence in food and said, "Well, now my soul feels alive!"

For you, studying, writing, and speaking may not put a wind in your sails. Maybe it's creating recipes, organizing a home or business, mentoring other

women, or helping others pursue healthier lives. We all have so many different passions and God-given abilities. The difficult thing is to remember God's character during those seasons when we are surrounded by life's manure.

Today we are going to look at God's name El Chay, the Living God. God reveals His character as El Chay only three times in Scripture. The first mention is in Joshua 3. We are fast-forwarding over some pretty key events after leaving Jacob's story of wrestling with God. Here's a quick summary of those events.

The people of Israel left the land of Canaan because of a famine and settled in Egypt where the Lord provided for them through Jacob's son Joseph. They eventually became slaves in Egypt and lived under oppression for over four hundred years. God raised up Moses to stand up to Pharaoh and lead His people out of Egypt. It was only an eleven-day journey to return to the Promised Land of Canaan, but they had a forty-year detour filled with wandering as a result of their complaining and rebellion. Eventually it was time to enter the land. The promise God made to Abraham was going to be fulfilled for his multitude of descendants. Joshua prepared the people to go into the land.

Extra Insight

The ark of the covenant was a chest built from wood and gold (Exodus 25:10-11) that contained a container of manna, the stone tablets with the Ten Commandments, and Aaron's staff that bloomed (Exodus 16:33-34; 25:10-16; Numbers 17:1-11).

Read Joshua 3 and answer the following questions:

What were the priests carrying for people to follow? (v. 3)

How is God described in verse 10?

What miracle did God perform in this chapter?

After forty years of wandering, the time had come for the people to prepare for battle. God spoke through Joshua, saying that on this day they would know the Living God (El Chay) was among them. It's possible they had never heard this name for God before, since this is the first mention of it in the Bible. This generation would have heard about the parting of the Red Sea, but God showed them His mighty power firsthand. He wanted them to know that He wasn't dead. He is El Chay, the Living God.

Have there been seasons in your life when God has seemed to be more at work in your life than in other seasons? Describe a time when God's presence and power were unmistakable in your life.

Perhaps you wrote about the birth of a child, a breakthrough in your finances, or a difficult season when you felt God's comfort. God is alive and at work! Other times in our lives, we go through dry seasons when we struggle to make sense of the spiritual numbness we experience.

During winter in Ohio, where I live, most of the trees look dead. They have no leaves or signs of life. Yet every spring, new signs of life come, and the growth and blooms are breathtaking. I imagine that the forty years in the wilderness might have felt like perpetual winter for the Israelites, yet at the banks of the Jordan they saw the promise of new life. When God parted the waters as the Levitical priests stood in the water, El Chay made His presence known in a huge way. In Joshua 4, we see that the Lord instructed the people to set up twelve stones to make a memorial. They were to remember this day when the Living God did something amazing so that on the dark days they wouldn't forget. You may not have seen actual waters part, but it's important to remember those times when we have experienced God's power and presence.

What are some things that help you remember the Living God during "winter" seasons of faith?

We may not set up stones, but we can find our own memorial methods so that we remember God is alive even when we don't see or sense Him at work. One of the members of the pilot study group shared that her memorial stones are found in an odd place. Facebook memories often pop up photos from when her son went through chemotherapy. He has been cancer-free for five years, and those pictures cause her to praise God for how He sustained her family during that season. Other women in the group shared these ideas:

- Put Scripture verses on sticky notes in prominent places such as in the car, bathroom, kitchen, or on the phone. Sticky notes can serve as memorial stones in our modern lives!
- Sing songs, especially ones that highlight God's character.
- Walk in nature. When we can't feel God, we can go look at what He made and see His work.
- Look at special items that help us remember a person or truth. One woman talked about a plate that says "JOY," which was a gift everyone in her Bible study received that reminds her of the joy of knowing God. Another woman mentioned a poster from a conference with a theme that especially resonated with her. She put it on her fridge to remember how close she felt to the Lord at that time.

These are just a few examples of things that can help us to remember what God did in the past so we can trust Him in the present—especially on the days when we want quick fixes. The easy comforts the world promises will ultimately not bring us life. We must continually push past our desire for instant gratification so we can pursue the living God with practices we know will help us remember that He is El Chay, the Living God.

Let's take a brief look at the other two passages where we find the name El Chay.

Read the following verses and underline the phrase "Living God."

"Yet the time will come when Israel's people will be like the sands of the seashore—too many to count! Then, at the place where they were told, 'You are not my people,' it will be said, 'You are children of the living God.'"

(Hosea 1:10)

I thirst for God, the living God.
When can I go and stand before him?
(Psalm 42:2)

The prophet Hosea spoke of the Abrahamic covenant that we have studied this week. God said the whole world would be blessed through Abraham. That includes you and me. We have the opportunity to be called children of El Chay, the Living God. The psalmist said he had a thirst for the Living God. I'm asking myself, *Do I thirst for the Living God?* Do you? If you couldn't think of any memorials of faith to remember the Living God, here is an option for you. Memorize Psalm 42:2 above. When we memorize God's Word, it increases the Holy Spirit's vocabulary in our lives. We can remember God is alive when we meditate on this verse, especially during dry seasons.

I can imagine that Jesus's disciples experienced a confusing season when Jesus died on the cross. How could the Son of God be dead? Yet we know that three days later, He rose again! When life seems confusing like it must have been for the disciples on the Friday when Jesus died, we too can remember that Sunday is coming.

He is El Chay, the Living God. On our darkest days, we thirst for the Living God. When we feel stuck, our circumstances may seem to parallel that bird stuck in the manure. These are the days when we must remember that our lives have seasons. We can thirst for God and hold on to His promises. And we can set up memorials to remember that God is alive and at work, even when we can't see it.

Behold

Today we have beheld El Chay, the Living God who parts waters and does big things in our lives.

Believe

Write a statement of belief:

God, I believe you are _____ in my life. I believe You

can _____ .

Bloom

As you think about the seasons of the spiritual life below, put a star by the one that most resembles your current season of faith. Don't overthink these options. Just reflect for a few moments and pick one.

_____ FALL   The leaves are changing in preparation.

_____ WINTER   Things seem dead and lifeless right now.

_____ SPRING   You can see the buds of new life as you
                    anticipate what is ahead.

_____ SUMMER   Your faith is in full bloom as you see the fruit of
                    what God is doing.

Now write a simple prayer below, asking God to show Himself alive to you no matter what season of faith you find yourself in.

It can be tempting to want to rush out of winter seasons. Or perhaps we just want to get through them with quick fixes. Don't let a worldly cat that just wants to harm you dig you out of the hard season. Some of those things we think will help us in the moment will actually bring death to our relationships, thought life, and our very souls. Remember the Living God has done great things before, and He will do it again. Hold on to those memorials of faith when you were sure of His presence and keep thirsting for the Living God in every season.

Talk with God

El Chay, You are the Living God. Give me perspective regarding the seasons of spiritual life. You are alive and working even when everything feels dark and difficult. Show me where You are working around me so that my faith in You can be strengthened today. Amen.

Big Idea

We can cling to the presence and power of El Chay, the Living God, rather than look for quick fixes during dark seasons.

Memory Verse Exercise

Read the Memory Verse on page 42 several times, and then fill in the blanks below as you recite it:

¹ _____ who _____ ____ the _____ _____ the _____
_____ [El Elyon]
____ _____ _____ ___ the _____ of the
_____ [El Shaddai].
² _____ I _____ _____ the _____:
____ _____ is _____ _____, my _____ of _____;
_____ is _____ _____, _____ I _____ _____.

(Psalm 91:1-2)

Weekly Wrap Up

Review the Big Idea for each day, and then write any personal application that comes to mind.

Day 1: El Shaddai—All-Sufficient One
Big Idea: When we recognize El Shaddai's sufficiency, we can pursue greater dependency.

Personal Application:_____

_____

Day 2: El Shaddai—Promise Keeper
Big Idea: We can wait patiently knowing that El Shaddai will fulfill every promise He has made.

Personal Application:_____

_____

Day 3: El Olam—Everlasting God
Big Idea: We live within the framework of time and look to El Olam to help us manage it wisely.

Personal Application:_____

_____

Day 4: El-Elohe-Israel—The God of Me
Big Idea: The Mighty God of the Universe is also the God of me.

Personal Application:_____

_____

Day 5: El Chay—Living God
Big Idea: We can cling to the presence and power of El Chay, the
             Living God, rather than look for quick fixes during dark
             seasons.

Personal Application:_____

_____

Video Viewer Guide: Week 2

When we recognize God's _____, then we can pursue greater

_____.

El Shaddai is our source for _____.

Genesis 17:1-6

El Shaddai is our source for _____.

Genesis 35:9-12

El Shaddai is the source of our _____.

Genesis 43:14

El Shaddai is the source of _____.

Genesis 49:25

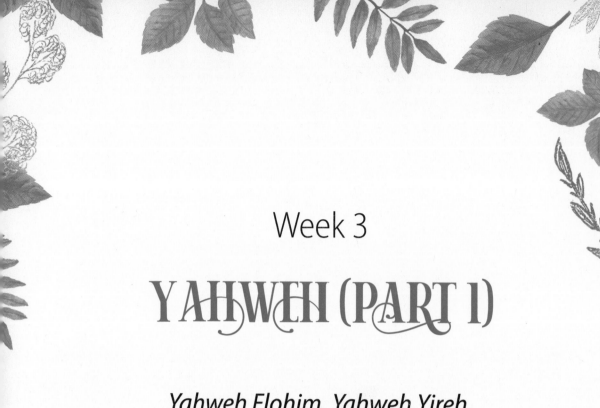

Week 3

YAHWEH (PART 1)

Yahweh Elohim, Yahweh Yireh,
Yahweh Rapha, Yahweh Nissi

Memory Verse

God also said to Moses, "Say this to the people of Israel: Yahweh, the God of your ancestors—the God of Abraham, the God of Isaac, and the God of Jacob—has sent me to you.

> *This is my eternal name,*
> *my name to remember for all generations."*

(Exodus 3:15)

Day 1: Yahweh Elohim—Unchanging God

One day I read a recipe so intently that I didn't notice the onions I had just put into a pan on the stove were burning. Another time I got so focused on the email I was writing that I didn't hear my daughter calling for me in the next room. When I focus on yard work, I tend to ignore tidying the inside of my house.

Can you think of a time when you became caught up in one thing to the neglect of another? Write anything that comes to mind below:

Scripture Focus

Genesis 2:4; 3; Deuteronomy 4:35; 6:4; Psalm 19:1-9, 14

Maybe you got cleaning done but didn't have time to prepare dinner. Perhaps at work you put your energy into a future project and weren't able to complete your daily assignments. We can't possibly give our full attention to everything at the same time, so often we must prioritize our attention. But when it comes to knowing God's character, the stakes are much higher. Today we will find that when we over-focus on one aspect of God's nature to the exclusion of another, it can skew our theology.

For the last two weeks we have focused on the El names of God. This week we will begin a two-week emphasis on the Yahweh names. Before we delve into the meaning of Yahweh, I want you to see the cohesion between the El names and the Yahweh names. Tomorrow we will spend more time unpacking Yahweh's meaning and significance, but today we will look for places in Scripture where Yahweh and Elohim are used together in order to see God's unchanging nature.

During biblical times, most religions of the nations surrounding Israel were polytheistic, which meant they incorporated many gods into their spiritual practices. The Old Testament concept of monotheism—the worship of one God—set the people of Israel apart from most of their neighbors. The Israelites' different names for God didn't represent multiple gods but highlighted diverse aspects of God's character.

Not long after creating the entire world, God revealed Himself as Yahweh. In Genesis 2:4 we encounter the name Yahweh for the first time, used in combination with Elohim.

Read Genesis 2:4 in the margin and write the English names used for God below:

Extra Insight

"Jehovah" was first used by the Masoretes, who read the vowels of Adonai in YHWH. The more accurate pronunciation is Yahweh.[1]

This is the account of the creation of the heavens and the earth. When the LORD God made the earth and the heavens.
(Genesis 2:4)

_____   _____

Yahweh is often translated in our English versions using the word Lord in a capital and small capital letters. Elohim is usually translated "God." Yahweh Elohim, the LORD God, made the earth and the heavens. This isn't a different God from the first chapter of Genesis. As we are learning, God's names highlight particular elements of His character. Elohim reveals God's mighty power as Creator while Yahweh is the more personal name for God.

Most references in Genesis 2 include the name Yahweh Elohim, emphasizing both God's power and relational nature.

Read Genesis 3:1-19, taking note of the names used for God. Fill in the chart with either Elohim, Yahweh, or Yahweh Elohim according to the key. (I filled in a few tricky ones for you!)

KEY	English Translation	Hebrew
	LORD	Yahweh
	God	Elohim
	LORD God	Yahweh Elohim

Verse	English and Hebrew Names for God	Speaker
1	God / Elohim	Serpent
3		Eve
5		Serpent
8		n/a
9		God to Adam
11	LORD God / Yahweh Elohim	God to Adam and Eve
13		God to Eve
14		God to serpent

Extra Insight

Yahweh's name appears more than 6,800 times in the Bible, making it the most used name for God.[2]

We don't know for sure, but what guesses could you make regarding why the serpent omitted the name Yahweh and referred to God solely as Elohim?

Answers: v. 3 God / Elohim, v. 5 God / Elohim, v. 8 LORD God / Yahweh Elohim, v. 9 LORD God / Yahweh Elohim, v. 13 LORD God / Yahweh Elohim, v. 14 LORD God, Yahweh Elohim

Some Bible teachers have pointed out that the serpent, which scholars have traditionally interpreted as symbolizing Satan, might have purposely emphasized God's power and control rather than His personal relationship with His creation by omitting Yahweh and just using Elohim.[3] While this is only opinion, we can see the danger of emphasizing one aspect of God's character to the exclusion of another. When we narrow our view of Him, we can open ourselves up to errors in judgment. It happened with Eve, and we too must be careful. God is:

- Just   but also Merciful
- Holy   but accessible through Christ
- Mighty in power   but abounding in Grace

These are just three examples. If we focus only on God's justice, we might forget His mercy. If we lose sight of Christ's compassion, we might start thinking of Him as cold and distant.

What dangers have you observed or personally encountered from overemphasizing one aspect of God's character without the balance of another aspect?

When he questioned Eve about the forbidden fruit, the serpent used the name for God's plurality and power but not His personal relationship with people. (Isn't that in keeping with the deceptive nature of our enemy to emphasize God's power and judgment and ignore God's gracious love?) Church history is loaded with examples of serpent-like behavior of Scripture-bullying people with half-truths about God. As we study God's names, we won't find God evolving or changing, but we will grow deeper in our understanding of His character. As we look at how Yahweh and Elohim are coupled in Scripture, we gain greater clarity about His personal desire to interact with His creations—even after they have disobeyed Him.

Take a moment to reread Genesis 3:15. Theologians refers to this verse as the *proto-evangelium*,[5] a long word for the first hint of God's Messianic plan in the Bible. Certainly, the original audience didn't understand that Jesus would be Eve's offspring that would strike Satan's head. Through progressive revelation we can look back with greater clarity and see that the moment sin cursed the planet, Yahweh Elohim had a plan for redemption. Sin separated us from perfect relationship with our Creator, and our mighty and personal God sent His Son to restore us. Knowing God's names helps us grasp His character. His power *and* love come through clearly as we read that He is Yahweh Elohim.

Extra Insight

Yahweh appears in every book in the Old Testament except Esther, Ecclesiastes, and Song of Solomon.[4]

Moses spelled it out clearly when he essentially said that Yahweh is Elohim. He reviewed what God had done for His people and then said, "He showed you these things so you would know that the Lord [Yahweh] is God [Elohim] and there is no other" (Deuteronomy 4:35).

Psalm 19 is another great example of a text where we find the names Elohim and Yahweh revealing different sides of God's character.

> Read the verses below and underline any references to Elohim (God). Circle references to Yahweh (LORD). Remember to mark pronouns such as "his" or "him" that refer to either of these names. I have done the first two verses for you.

¹The heavens proclaim the glory of _God_.

The skies display _his_ craftsmanship.

²Day after day they continue to speak;

night after night they make _him_ known.

³They speak without a sound or word;

their voice is never heard.

⁴Yet their message has gone throughout the earth,

and their words to all the world.

God has made a home in the heavens for the sun.

⁵It bursts forth like a radiant bridegroom after his wedding.

It rejoices like a great athlete eager to run the race.

⁶The sun rises at one end of the heavens

and follows its course to the other end.

Nothing can hide from its heat.

⁷The instructions of the Lord are perfect,

reviving the soul.

The decrees of the Lord are trustworthy,

making wise the simple.

⁸The commandments of the Lord are right,

bringing joy to the heart.

giving insight for living.

⁹Reverence for the Lord is pure,

lasting forever.

The laws of the Lord are true;

each one is fair.

(Psalm 19:1-9)

What differences do you notice in the verses referring to Elohim and Yahweh?

First we see Elohim as Creator who made the heavens, sky, and sun. Then the psalmist transitions, using Yahweh to focus on God's laws and instructions. These commands help us know how to interact and revere our God. God's character never changes; it simply can't be contained in only one name. We want to grow our view of God so that we don't emphasize one aspect of His nature to the neglect of another. He is mighty *and* relational.

As I look back over the course of my life, I see growth and change. I am in a state of becoming. Yahweh is not like us in this respect. He isn't learning along the way. Yahweh's Son shares this quality.

Read Hebrews 13:8 in the margin and write below what you learn about God's unchanging nature:

Jesus Christ is the same yesterday, today, and forever.
(Hebrews 13:8)

Jesus is the same yesterday, today, and forever, and He wants to help us be more conformed to His image. The better we understand that image, the better we can cooperate with the Spirit and grow into it. The writer of Psalm 19 ends the chapter with a desire to be more like Yahweh. Let's end our time together praying these words:

> *May the words of my mouth*
> *and the meditation of my heart*
> *be pleasing to you,*
> *O LORD, my rock and my redeemer.*
> (Psalm 19:14)

Yahweh is our Rock and Redeemer, and He always will be. When we behold and believe Yahweh, we can bloom with tremendous growth.

Behold

The names Yahweh and Elohim highlight different aspects of the character of our unchanging God.

Believe

Write a statement of belief:

Because Yahweh is a personal God, I believe He_____

_____.

Bloom

As we see Yahweh's unchanging nature, we find a firm foundation in the midst of our changing circumstances. He is our Rock and Redeemer. End today taking some time to reflect on Yahweh Elohim and ask the Lord to transform your words and the meditations of your heart.

Talk with God

Yahweh Elohim, You are both powerful and personal. Help me not to lose sight of who You really are. I want to know You. Thank You for being an unchanging God. Please show me how the words of my mouth and the meditations of my heart can be pleasing in Your sight today! Amen.

Memory Verse Exercise

Read the Memory Verse on page 76 several times, and then fill in the blanks below as you recite it:

God also _____ to Moses, "Say this to the _____ of Israel: _____, the God of your ancestors—the God of Abraham, the God of Isaac, and the God of Jacob—has sent me to you.

> *This is my eternal name,*
>   *my name to remember for all generations."*

                                                   (Exodus 3:15)

Big Idea

Yahweh never changes, and the name Yahweh Elohim highlights God's personal relationship with us.

Day 2: Yahweh—The Self-Existent One

Scripture Focus

Exodus 3:1-15

When my youngest child, Rachel, was born, my son was just starting kindergarten and my twin daughters were two years old. To say I was a little overwhelmed in that season would be an understatement. When Rachel's birth certificate came in the mail, I noticed that it said she was born on the second of the month, but she actually was born on the fifth. I made a mental note to look into getting that changed but got swept up in tantrums, diaper changes, potty-training, and reading lessons. Years went by and I didn't think much about it until one day when she was in middle school and she wanted to go on a mission trip. Guess what she needed? Yep, a passport. I realized we didn't have time to get a new birth certificate in time to apply for the needed passport.

I asked Rachel what she thought about having two birthdays—a real one and a "paperwork" one. She bargained for cake on both days, and I assured her she would have a great story to tell when she needed to come up with an interesting fact about herself. Even if her birth certificate has the wrong day on it, we know when Rachel entered the world!

When were you born? If you have been told any stories about that day, summarize them briefly below. (You don't have to write the year down if you don't want to.)

Extra Insight

"The Tetragrammaton is the combination of four Hebrew letters to form the ancient Hebrew name of God, YHWH. This name demonstrates God's self-existence and self-sufficiency and is linked to how God described himself to Moses."[6]

Yahweh has no birthdate. Someone chose a day in December to celebrate the day Jesus put on flesh and came to earth, but our God has no beginning or end. He always has been, and He always will be. Yahweh comes from four Hebrew consonants that form a tetragrammaton YHWH.

Here are a few fun facts about the name Yahweh to keep in mind as we study:

- The name YHWH was considered so holy that even scribes didn't say it out loud.
- Later, vowels from the name Adonai (which we will study later) were added to form the name Yahweh when people began to speak this name aloud.
- Scholars in the Middle Ages were the first to translate Yahweh with the English rendering Jehovah.[7]
- Many English translations use the word LORD in all capitals for Yahweh.

Most scholars associate YHWH with the verb "to be," so this name is sometimes defined as "the self-existent One."[8] Yahweh has always been and is completely self-sustaining and self-sufficient. Today we'll look at an encounter with Yahweh in the Book of Exodus that reveals more about His character.

Exodus means "exit." After God's people had been enslaved in Egypt for over four hundred years, God called a man named Moses to lead them to a new land. Moses was alone in a wilderness when he saw a bush burning but not being consumed. (Imagine firewood burning in a fire pit but never turning to ash.)

Read Exodus 3:1-15 and write how God describes Himself to Moses in verse 6:

God is the God of Abraham, Isaac, and Jacob. I hope you recognize those names of the patriarchs, which we've encountered as we've studied God's names woven into their stories. So far we've learned these traits of God through His names:

- Elohim—Creator
- El Elyon—God Most High
- El Roi—The God Who Sees Me
- El Shaddai—All-Sufficient One
- El Olam—Everlasting God
- El Chay—Living God

Moses would have been familiar with these names through the oral tradition of storytelling. He knew the greatness of God through his ancestors Abraham, Isaac, and Jacob. Yet like us he had to reconcile the truths about God with his circumstantial fears. Try for a moment to put yourself in Moses's shoes. God asked him to demand that Pharaoh, the most powerful man in the world at the time, release his entire workforce. Based on the census in the Book of Numbers, we are likely talking about over a million people. I can understand why Moses had some questions for Yahweh.

What questions did Moses ask of God in Exodus 3:11 and 3:13?

1.

2.

How did God answer these questions in Exodus 3:12 and 3:14?

1.

2.

Moses had two questions for God: *Who am I?* and *Who are you?* These two questions are rooted in identity. We must know our identity as well as God's identity in order to carry out His instructions in our lives. God assured Moses that he didn't need special abilities or status. Yahweh's presence and promise were enough in spite of Moses's perceived shortcomings.

While I've never seen a burning bush or heard the audible voice of God calling me with specific instructions, I have sensed the Holy Spirit nudging me to encourage others, write Bible studies, and teach the Bible in my local church. Instructions such as those can be scary. When I first sensed God's call to use my gifts to serve the Lord, I remember thinking to myself, *Who do you think you are?* I knew so many godly people who could do what God was calling me to do so much better. My insecurities only grew when I shared my heart with a dear friend. I thought she would respond with encouragement, but instead she said that perhaps I should just focus on being a wife and a mother. It felt to me like she was echoing the voice inside that said, *Who do you think you are?*

I heard someone say recently that insecurity is an intruder in the house of wisdom. It certainly was in mine. It delayed my obedience to God's call. As I wrestled through my doubts and fears, I came to understand that serving God is not about who "can." Often it is about who "will." I sensed God asking, "Will you?" I had to decide if I would pursue what I felt the Lord calling me to do— with or without the support of my friend, with or without a sign of how it would all turn out, with or without complete clarity in the process. Ultimately knowing that Yahweh is "I AM" quells all of our excuses.

Have you had a season when you wrestled with God regarding next steps to take in serving Him? If so, write about it briefly:

You may not be called to free slaves like Moses or write Bible studies like me, but God has given each Christ-follower spiritual gifts and abilities to use in His service. Perhaps He has called you to serve in children's ministry, lead a Bible study, encourage others with hand-written notes, coordinate meals, create beautiful spaces for worship, or do an endless number of other things to bring glory to God. Remember Elohim is creative, and we are made in His image. There is no limit to the ways the Lord will use our unique abilities to bring Him glory.

What gifts or abilities are you currently using to serve God?

If nothing comes to mind, spend a few minutes asking the Lord for direction in how and where He has called you to follow Him in this season. Then listen for any thoughts or ideas that come to mind, and record them below:

Like Moses, you may not feel like you are equipped to do anything for God. The Lord told Moses that His presence and His promise were all that was needed to take the next step of obedience in faith. I love it that even after these assurances, Moses still had another question. He wanted to know what name he should give to the people. God told him to say "I AM" had sent him.

What does the expression for God "I AM" reveal about His character?

When Moses needed confirmation, Yahweh said, "Whatever you need, I AM."
If you need a provider, I AM
If you need help, I AM
If you need deliverance, I AM

What are some excuses people might have for not obeying God's call in their lives?

God says that regardless of whatever we truly need to obey Him, we can trust that He is "I AM." He will supply all that we need to follow His specific path. He is self-existent. This means He isn't dependent on anything or anyone. Like the sun doesn't need an outside source of fire to stay hot, Yahweh doesn't need anything or anyone to sustain Him.

I love that Yahweh didn't get exasperated with Moses for revealing insecurities and asking questions. Instead, He helped him and assured him of His power.

What does Exodus 3:15 reveal about the name Yahweh?

This is our memory verse for the week. Meditating on it will anchor in our minds the truth that Yahweh is eternal and His name is for all generations, including this one. We can rest assured that our God has no limitations. Moses went on to display God's power through miraculous plagues and a supernatural parting of the Red Sea. He had to trust Yahweh each step of the way, continuing to ask for assurance about his own identity and God's ability to use him. We can trust that Yahweh will direct us too and give us all that we need to accomplish His instructions. He is the great I AM.

Behold

Yahweh is the great I AM who is self-existent.

Believe

Answer the two following questions Moses asked by filling in the blanks. (There are no right or wrong answers here!)

I am _____ because Yahweh is with me.

Yahweh is _____, so I can follow His instructions in my life knowing that His presence and promises will guide me.

Bloom

When we behold and believe that Yahweh is the God of our present, we can bloom knowing that He will guide us today.

If you encountered a burning bush right now, what do you think the Lord would be asking you to do? Record any ideas below:

Talk with God

Yahweh, You are the self-existent One. When I look at my deficiencies, I feel so ill-equipped to serve You. Help me instead to focus on who You are and who I am in You. Give me Your strength and power to boldly serve You. Show me where You want to use my gifts to build others up so that I might honor You in this season of my life. Amen.

Memory Verse Exercise

Read the Memory Verse on page 76 several times, and then fill in the blanks below as you recite it:

God also _____ to Moses, "Say this to the _____ of Israel: _____, the God of your _____—the God of _____, the God of _____, and the God of _____—has sent me to you.

   This is my eternal name,
      my name to remember for all generations."

                                        (Exodus 3:15)

Day 3: Yahweh Yireh—The Lord Will Provide

Earlier this week we studied a compound name for God, Yahweh Elohim. Over the next two weeks we will discover many names coupled with Yahweh that reveal specific character traits of our personal God. Yireh means "to see."[9] "The English word *provision* is made up of two Latin words that mean 'to see

Big Idea

Yahweh needs nothing from an outside source and has no beginning or end.

Scripture Focus

Genesis 22:1-19

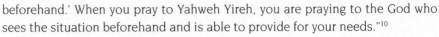

Yahweh Yireh
is sometimes
translated in English
as "Jehovah Jireh."
For the sake of
continuity, we will
use the original
form "Yahweh Yireh"
in referring to this
compound name
for God.

God never tempts
us (James 1:13), but
He *tested* Abraham's
faith (Genesis 22:1;
Hebrews 11:17).

beforehand.' When you pray to Yahweh Yireh, you are praying to the God who sees the situation beforehand and is able to provide for your needs."[10]

When I asked on social media for people to share stories of how God has provided in their lives, the response was overwhelming. People wrote responses of God's provision of needed resources, people, or answers they were seeking. Here are three that I found especially compelling:

We lost our daughter last year. Due to the hospital bills and extenuating circumstances, buying a proper headstone for her wasn't something we could consider. A family in our church stepped up and paid for it in full as a way to support our journey through grief.

Things were really tight, and I was at the grocery with my two small children. I had $20 to get our groceries for the next two weeks. A stranger walked up to me and handed me a grocery store gift card with $200 on it and provided the next several weeks' worth of groceries for our family of four.

I longed for a mother figure in my life and was feeling saddened by not having a maternal figure to help guide me through the early marriage and raising young children years. As I was mourning, God began to turn that mourning into gratefulness as He provided other women to fill in the gaps in different ways. I realized that God did indeed provide for me, just in a different way than I had originally wanted.

As you reflect on your life, how have you seen Yahweh Yireh provide in your life? Share one or two examples that stand out.

The first mention of Yahweh Yireh appears in Genesis when Abraham's promised son, Isaac, was a growing boy.

Read Genesis 22:1-19 and answer the following questions:

What was God's intent according to verse 1?

What did the Lord instruct Abraham to do? (v. 2)

How did Abraham respond? (v. 3)

What did Abraham say to his servant? (v. 5)

At what point in the process did the Lord stop Abraham? (vv. 10-11)

What was the angel's message for Abraham? (v. 12)

How did the Lord provide an offering? (v. 13)

What name for God is mentioned in verse 14?

When the angel called to Abraham again, what blessings were mentioned? (vv. 15-18)

What thoughts or questions stood out to you as you read this passage?

Extra Insight

"Moriah, the site of Abraham's thwarted attempt to sacrifice his son, has been traditionally associated with the temple mount in Jerusalem. Today Mount Moriah is occupied by a Muslim shrine called the Dome of the Rock."[11]

I marveled at the theological contradiction for Abraham. What God was asking him to do ran contrary to God's promise for a future nation. In the first week of our study we learned about God's special covenant with Abraham to bless him and give him a multitude of descendants (Genesis 12). When more than a decade went by, Abraham and Sarah decided to help God by using their servant Hagar as a surrogate. Eventually they had the son of promise in their old age. In today's reading, we find the Lord asking Abraham to kill this very son.

Abraham's response wasn't delayed. The text doesn't record any bargaining or questioning like what we saw from Moses yesterday. This incident reveals that Abraham trusted God completely. We get a little more insight in the New Testament.

Read Hebrews 11:17-19 and write below what we learn about Abraham's reasoning:

"For this is how God loved the world: He gave his one and only Son, so that everyone who believes in him will not perish but have eternal life."
(John 3:16)

Since he did not spare even his own Son but gave him up for us all, won't he also give us everything else?
(Romans 8:32)

For God's will was for us to be made holy by the sacrifice of the body of Jesus Christ, once for all time.
(Hebrews 10:10)

The writer of Hebrews tells us that Abraham reasoned that God would raise Isaac from the dead if necessary. I believe it is no coincidence that the first time we see Yahweh Yireh's name used, it is with a father offering up his son.

Read the New Testament verses in the margin and write below what they tell us about God's own sacrifice:

Take a moment to consider what God has provided for you through Christ. Sin separated us from God, but Christ laid down His life as a sacrifice, enduring the cross with its physical pain and emotional insults, and taking our sin upon Himself. Jesus is the ultimate expression of Yahweh Yireh in reconciling our relationship with God through His willing sacrifice. No angel intervened to stop the sacrifice as He bled and died for us.

As we think about the name Yahweh Yireh, we want to express our gratitude for the ultimate provision He has made in our lives. Write a brief prayer below thanking God for sending Christ on your behalf:

Yahweh Yireh provided His only Son, but He also cares about moms in the grocery store who need food for their children and women who grew up without a mother. He knows about the answers you seek regarding your health, or the loneliness you may be experiencing while desiring a life partner, or restoration in your marriage or other relationship. He is a provider and longs to take care of your needs.

Write below what you are asking God to provide in your life currently:

Whether we need resources, direction, people, or information, Yahweh Yireh stands ready to provide for us. The questions I have to ask myself when it comes to my needs are these:

- How can I obey any instructions the Lord gives me regarding my need?

- Will I trust Him to provide?
- Are there any limits to my obedience?

Abraham didn't delay in believing and acting on God's commands. Sometimes I want God's help in doing things my way. I doubt Him when the timing and provision don't line up with my expectations. From Abraham's example, I am challenged to completely surrender my needs into God's hands, trusting that He would even raise the dead to make it happen.

Yahweh Yireh provides for us in so many ways, but at times we fail to recognize and celebrate His gifts. A sweet friend shared with me that things were particularly difficult in her family's finances, interpersonal relationships, and ministry responsibilities. She decided her family needed to look closer to see God's provision in the midst of all the trials. She went to a dollar store and bought a plate, a tall candle, a hurricane glass candle cover, river rocks, and a marker. At the beginning of the project, all the rocks were on the plate outside the hurricane glass. Every time God provided in some way, a family member wrote the provision on a rock and put it inside the glass. Eventually her family couldn't see the candle anymore as the rocks piled high. This visible reminder served to help them see God as Yahweh Yireh. They began to look for God's provision in the big and little things. At the end of the year they read the rocks and remembered how the Lord had provided money, opportunities, or even things they had taken for granted such as clean water and healthy bodies.

Write one thing you are thankful for that God has provided in your life on each rock below:

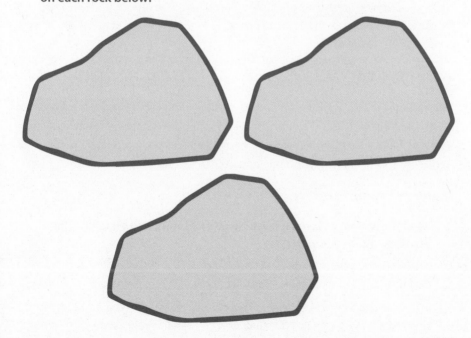

I'm grateful today for sunshine streaming through my window, my college daughter getting an opportunity to study in Israel next semester, and a new small group Bible study with young married couples that my husband and I are leading.

Yahweh Yireh isn't scrambling to take care of us. He doesn't have to take out loans or fret over how He will provide. He is a self-existent God. Scripture says He owns the cattle on a thousand hills (Psalm 50:10), meaning that His resources are unlimited. He sees your needs and longs for you to depend on Him for provision.

Behold

Yahweh Yireh is a God who provides.

Believe

Write a statement of belief:

Because He is Yahweh Yireh, I can trust Him to provide

_____ in my life.

Bloom

As we look for God's provision, we may notice things we had missed previously. If you are going through a hard time, consider my friend's idea of listing God's provision on rocks or some other creative method to recognize and appreciate Yahweh Yireh.

Talk with God

Yahweh Yireh, You are my Provider. So often I reach for tangible things because I can't see or feel You. Help me to trust You even when I feel numb to Your presence. Give me faith to trust that You are the true source when it comes to my finances, health, relationships, and every other need in my life. Thank You for revealing Your name as Yahweh Yireh! Amen.

Memory Verse Exercise

Read the Memory Verse on page 76 several times, and then fill in the blanks below as you recite it:

God also _____ to Moses, "Say this to the _____ of Israel: _____, the God of your _____—the God of _____, the God of _____, and the God of _____—has sent me to _____.

Big Idea

Yahweh Yireh sees our needs and provides resources, people, and information according to His timetable for our ultimate good rather than our immediate pleasure.

This is my _____ name,

my name to _____for all

_____."

(*Exodus 3:15*)

Day 4: Yahweh Rapha— The Lord Who Heals You

My friend Lee described the night when he lay alone on his hospital bed, feeling as though he were hanging over a cliff and the Lord asked him this question: "Will you trust me?" He wrestled to reconcile God's goodness with the direness of his circumstances. He was in his early forties with a brain tumor that was later diagnosed as glioblastoma.

The following days were a wilderness of surgery, medications, and recovery. Contrary to what doctors had told him, Lee got better, with no signs of cancer. He felt great and took every opportunity to share about God's miraculous healing in his life. After five years of excellent health, Lee told me at a church campout to pray for him because he was experiencing terrible headaches. The next week his suspicions were confirmed. The tumor was back and growing.

Our church family set up a prayer schedule to pray for him around the clock. Men from our church gathered on his front porch most nights singing worship songs and praying for him. I had the chance to sit with Lee in the final weeks of his life and take notes as he told his story of faith in order to write a short memoir of his experiences. Lee told me that he was a winner no matter how his cancer journey ended. If the Lord restored his health, he would have more time to spend with his family and to share God's story. If he died, then he would be with Jesus. "I can't lose," he told me. Within a few weeks Lee found ultimate healing as he entered heaven.

God's healing power leaves me with many questions such as:

- Why did God heal Lee the first time but not the second?
- Why does God heal some people and not others?
- Why is there so much physical, emotional, and mental suffering in our world?
- Why does God allow us to suffer?

What situations or questions come to mind when you think about healing?

Scripture Focus

Exodus 15:22-27

Pain and healing can be difficult topics. We want to celebrate God's healing power when we see it, but I believe we need caution in tying God's goodness to a desired result. Does it mean that He is bad or that we lacked faith when diseases progress or people die? God is good all the time—not just when we get the result we wanted.

One of the compound uses of Yahweh's name is Yahweh Rapha. Rapha means "to heal, make healthful." It is used sixty-two times in the Old Testament and can refer to the healing of persons, nations, individual distresses, water, and even possessions like pottery.[12]

The first mention of this name is found in Exodus. Exodus recounts the story of Moses helping God's people exit from slavery in Egypt. After ten plagues had devastated the land, the people of Israel were finally released, but they faced a problem on their journey to the Promised Land. The Red Sea blocked their path, and an Egyptian army was chasing them. God parted the water so the people could go through to dry land and the pursuing army drowned in the receding waters. After this incredible miracle, the community worshiped God with a song of praise that included these words:

> The LORD is my strength and my song;
>   he has given me victory.
> This is my God, and I will praise him—
>   my father's God, and I will exalt him!
>   (Exodus 15:2)

After their worship service ended, they began their journey through the wilderness and soon found the dry ground on the other side of the Red Sea to be very dry indeed.

Read Exodus 15:22-27, and match each phrase on the left with the corresponding word(s) on the right:

1. Days traveled without water (v. 22)	Oasis at Elim
2. Quality of the water at Marah (v. 23)	Wood
3. People's response to no water (v. 24)	Three
4. Object Moses threw into the water (v. 25)	Complaining
5. Condition of the promise (v. 26)	LORD who heals you
6. Name for God revealed (v. 26)	Obedience
7. Place they camped after Marah (v. 27)	Bitter

Answers: 1. Three 2. Bitter 3. Complaining 4. Wood 5. Obedience 6. LORD who heals you 7. Oasis at Elim

What stands out to you about this encounter?

One of the gals in the pilot study group said that what stands out most to her is that if we listen, we won't suffer as much. Another noticed that the people's spirits were bitter, like the water. I noticed that the Israelites had water problems. At the Red Sea, they had too much water that was blocking their way, and at Marah they lacked drinking water. While I'm inclined to be shocked by their complaining right on the heels of the Red Sea encounter, I know that often I doubt God. He has done amazing things in my life in the past, but when a different challenge arises, I often complain about the new obstacle. Can you relate?

The Israelites' need for healing was bitter water. Living on a broken planet means that we all need healing in many areas because sin's effects are widespread. Sin and sickness are related, but people like Lee don't get a brain tumor because of their personal sin. Nothing in Scripture supports that notion. Still, we do know that if sin had not entered the world, there would be no sickness or suffering. So there is a link between sin and sickness, but it is more general than specific. At times our personal sins can lead to sickness in our lives, but our ailments usually do not have one simple cause.

We know that Yahweh Rapha is a God who wants to heal our diseases. We tend to think of healing in terms of physical ailments, but we are broken in many ways: physically, sexually, emotionally, intellectually, relationally, and spiritually. Each of us needs spiritual healing through a relationship with Jesus Christ. All of us are born with the bitter waters of a sin nature. Jesus said this in John 7:38, "Anyone who believes in me may come and drink! For the Scriptures declare, 'Rivers of living water will flow from his heart.'" He is the only source for eternal healing in our lives.

If you have decided to follow Jesus, then you have experienced spiritual healing through Christ. Through His sacrifice and resurrection, He has restored your relationship with God.

Reflect now on times of healing in your past—spiritual, emotional, relational, physical, sexual, intellectual. Record anything that comes to mind below:

We need Yahweh Rapha's touch in every way. We can praise Him for how we have experienced His healing in the past, and yet we continue to cry out for healing because of our perpetual brokenness.

As you consider your life *right now*, what is your bitter water? In what situation do you currently need a touch from Yahweh Rapha?

Yahweh Rapha longs for us to experience ultimate healing. He also cares about the struggles we face each day. Much of life can feel like a wilderness journey. We are leaving the slavery of sin in the past and walking the journey of becoming more and more like Jesus through a process called sanctification. This refers to the progression of God conforming us into the image of His Son (Romans 8:29). We will never be sinless in this life, but we hope that over time we will sin less.

What purpose did the Lord mention for the bitter waters experience in Exodus 15:25-26?

Extra Insight

"Ferdidand de Lessups, builder of the Suez Canal, was told by Arab chiefs that they put a thorn bush into some types of water to make it palatable."[13] Whether the wood was symbolic or medicinal in some way, we see that God healed the water.

Yesterday we saw that the Lord tested Abraham's faith, and today we find that He tested the Israelites' faith between the Red Sea and the Promised Land. In other words, the dry conditions and bitter water provided an opportunity for them to exercise their faith. God performed miracles for the Israelites when there was too much water to get through and not enough water to drink, and both times He required His people to take a first step of faith. At the Red Sea, Moses had to pick up his staff, raise his hand over the sea, and tell the people to start moving before the waters parted (Exodus 14:15-16). At Marah, God instructed Moses to throw wood into the water to purify it. Throwing a piece of wood in the water didn't make logical sense, and many times the circumstances that test our faith don't either.

In Exodus 15:26, we read that God told the people of Israel to obey Him so that they would not experience the Egyptian diseases. This puzzled me at first because I know that Egyptians were considered one of the healthiest nations of antiquity.[14] They practiced cleanliness and good hygiene. Several commentators suggest that this reference to the diseases of the Egyptians has to do with the diseases brought on by sin and rebellion in their nation. Specifically, they suffered many plagues for their failure to heed Yahweh's commands. The Lord wanted to spare the Israelites from the pain associated with sin—and He wants to spare us from that as well. God is for us, not against us!

Look at Exodus 15:26 again. What were the conditions regarding the required response of God's people?

You may have worded it differently based on your translation, but basically the Lord asked His people to listen carefully to His voice, do what is right in His sight, obey His commands, and keep all of His decrees. These were the conditions given to avoid the Egyptian diseases of pride and rebellion. We too can experience Yahweh Rapha's healing power as we surrender our lives to Him.

Take a moment to consider any step of faith the Lord might be asking of you when it comes to the bitter water you noted on page 96. Is there a habit to break, a new practice to institute, a person to contact, an apology to offer, or another action step to take? Record what might be your "wood in the water" or a first step toward obedience:

Perhaps God is calling you to keep seeking answers. A friend of mine found her bitter water in declining health. She has always been an avid exerciser and healthy eater and couldn't understand the issue she was having with focus and fatigue. She didn't give up but continued talking to people, humbling herself under her limitations, and praying for God's wisdom. Eventually she got clarity as she discovered a huge group of women online who had similar experiences. After doing extensive research, she scheduled an operation. Two weeks after the procedure she is already experiencing relief.

The Lord calls us to play a role as we seek Him for healing. Though God does not cause our suffering, He does allow us to experience the realities of a broken world. And those circumstances often test or try our faith, helping us to learn more about God, strengthen our faith, and develop our character in the process.

How have times of testing in your life helped you to learn more about God, strengthen your faith, or develop your character?

When I went through a season of infertility, when my daughter had a life-threatening blood clot, and when another daughter lost her hair to alopecia, I grieved and prayed. Sometimes the Lord answered my prayers in the way I wanted, and other times He didn't. He is Yahweh Rapha, and He heals according to His plan and timetable. Today we can experience hope in the midst of our brokenness knowing that we serve a God who heals!

Behold

Yahweh Rapha is the Lord who heals us.

Believe

Write a statement of belief:

Because you are Yahweh Rapha, I believe you can heal

_____ as I _____.

Bloom

Take a moment to talk with Yahweh Rapha about the action step you identified above. Then to bolster your faith and help you take that step, spend a few moments identifying ways you previously have experienced God's healing touch in your life and family, whether physically, emotionally, relationally, or spiritually. Write them below:

We may not always understand God's decisions regarding healing. My friend Lee experienced physical healing and then ultimate healing. It didn't all make sense to those who loved him, but we can grow in faith through every difficult circumstance that tests our faith. Again, God does not cause our suffering but uses it to strengthen and prove our faith. Yahweh Rapha is the Lord who heals you. He wants to purify the bitter water in our lives, and He offers living water to quench our thirsty souls.

Talk with God

Yahweh Rapha, You know all my pain. I am broken in every way and in need of Your healing touch. Heal me from sin, disease, and brokenness today so that I might serve You with a whole heart and a willing mind. Help me to trust You even when my prayers aren't answered according to my desires and timing. I surrender myself into Your care as the God who heals me. Amen.

Memory Verse Exercise

Read the Memory Verse on page 76 several times, and then fill in the blanks on the following page as you recite it:

_____ also _____ to _____, "Say _____ to the _____ of _____: _____, the God of _____ _____—the God of _____, the God of _____, and the God of _____— has _____ ____ to _____.

> This is my _____ name,
>   my name to _____for all
> _____."

(Exodus 3:15)

Big Idea

Yahweh Rapha longs for each of us to experience ultimate healing.

Day 5: Yahweh Nissi—The Lord Our Banner

God showed Himself as our family's provider and a healer when my daughter spent fifteen days at a children's hospital fighting for her life. During her kindergarten year, she had a variety of puzzling symptoms that caused her organs to start shutting down with septic shock. During the days on the ventilator in the ICU, I felt God's presence and power in a way unparalleled to any other time in my life.

After the Lord provided incredible support from friends and family and healed our daughter in supernatural ways, I wasn't prepared for the battles I would face after going home. My other children had been displaced during the long ordeal and needed extra attention. My daughter was getting better but still required daily shots in her stomach because of a blood clot that resulted from a central line IV. To say I was weary would have been an understatement. But the crazy thing was the battle going on in my mind. I had stood firm in faith in the midst of the scary parts of the journey, but now that things were mostly better, I began replaying the original incident over and over in my mind. What if I had gone to the ER sooner? What if she hadn't been misdiagnosed for nine hours in the ER? What if I had pressed harder with questions and advocated harder for her in the early days of her symptoms? I knew that playing out these scenarios accomplished nothing, yet I was plagued with a battle in my mind.

Have you ever experienced a mental, spiritual, or emotional battle during a particularly weary season in life? Record anything that comes to mind below:

Scripture Focus

Exodus 17:8-16

Extra Insights

Nissi describes a flag or a banner. The idea is that God is victorious in battle and the flag of His victory is lifted high. The same word is used of the serpent on the pole in Numbers 21:8, and is also found in Psalm 60:4 and Isaiah 11:10.[15]

Amalek was the grandson of Jacob's brother Esau. The family feud between Jacob and Esau trickled down through the generations, with the Amalekites attacking Israel in the wilderness. Amalek was the first and constant enemy of Israel.

Today we will study a name of God that helps us to trust God's character and stand firm when we find ourselves in the midst of a battle: Yahweh Nissi, the Lord Our Banner. The first mention of this name is found in Exodus 17. After the people of Israel crossed the Red Sea, sang a song of praise, and complained about bitter water, they stood face-to-face with an enemy army. They were weary from travel and harsh conditions. The Lord had solved their water problem at Marah, and the people encountered a similar need for water at a placed called Rephidim. There the water was not bitter but nonexistent. Once again, the people complained, argued, and questioned God. They were asking a question we also can be tempted to ask: *Where is God when I need Him most?*

When we find ourselves here, we can complain or we can seek God. The Lord heard the complaints of the people and instructed Moses to strike a rock. Water supernaturally gushed out to meet their needs, showing the people God's provision and patience with them. Let's pick up the story in Exodus 17.

Read Exodus 17:8-16 and summarize the scenario in your own words below, perhaps imagining that you are telling the story to a group of children or teens or a friend:

It seems like the people of Israel can't catch a break. They were weary from traveling. They had endured several water emergencies. Now they have to go into battle. Remember that they had been slaves in Egypt for over four hundred years, making bricks and doing manual labor. They didn't have any experience with wilderness travel or battle. I love the lesson here for us about weak moments. We all have them. When we are hungry, angry, lonely, or tired, we often are called to battle. While we may not have a physical army in front of us, we are battling bad habits, addictions, and choices.

What are some temptations you face in your weak moments?

I tend to make bad food and media choices in my weary moments. I also find my fuse much shorter and my words less kind. Here are three practical lessons we will camp on today:

- We need to raise a banner during weak moments.
- We can't win our battles alone.
- Prayer and action are necessary to win our battles.

In Scripture, a banner was an object that represented something greater. In Numbers, each tribe and family was organized under banners.

Look again at Exodus 17:9. What was the "banner" that Moses raised on the mountain?

This was the same staff that Moses used to display God's power. Scripture mentions that this staff was . . .

- carried by Moses when he returned to Egypt to beseech Pharaoh (Exodus 4:20),
- thrown down in front of Pharaoh and turned into a snake (Exodus 7:10),
- raised high to initiate several of the plagues (Exodus 7:19; 8:5, 16; 9:23; 10:13),
- raised over the Red Sea to part the waters (Exodus 14:16), and
- used to strike the rock and provide water at Rephidim (Exodus 17:5-6).

The staff didn't have magical power, but it did represent the power of God. This "banner" was an object to lift high so that, during a weary season of battle, the people could remember that God had performed supernatural works in the past to give them strength in the present!

What are some of the works of God you recall from your past? Record a few on the banners below:

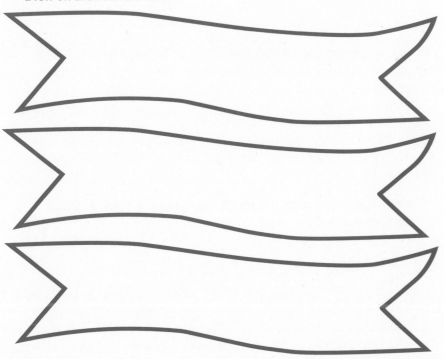

A banner of God's work in the past helps us believe Him for the present and future. The people were to look up at Moses's staff and remember the plagues, the Red Sea, and the water they drank out of a rock. Then they would know that God was bigger than their enemy. God revealed Himself as Yahweh Nissi, the Lord Our Banner. Like a flag that represents a nation, God wants us to set our eyes on symbols or reminders of His power rather than the strength of the enemy or our own personal weariness.

What are some tangible ways you can raise a banner of faith?

Honestly, I struggle with weak moments. I want to check out and give into temptation when I feel weary. Some things that have helped me raise a banner of faith include calling a friend and asking for prayer, memorizing or meditating on a Scripture, writing in a journal, and sleeping.

By bringing our battles into the light, we can experience more victory. We notice that the Israelites were in the battle together. When we fight alongside others, we can strengthen one another.

According to Exodus 17:12, how did Moses continue to raise the banner when he could hold his hands up no longer?

When Moses's legs and arms became weak, his brother Aaron and another man named Hur brought him to a stone to sit down. I love the picture of them bringing Moses to a stone. His friends brought him to a firm place to rest. "Rock" is another name used of God in the Bible. We can point our friends to Jesus, the solid ground, when they are weak. When they can't stand firm on the rock, we can lead them to sit on the rock of Christ while we stand alongside. Aaron and Hur also held up Moses's arms so that he could complete the work the Lord had for him.

Who has directed you to Jesus and supported you in some of your challenges in life?

Sometimes my pride keeps me from reaching out when I'm weary. I didn't want to tell anyone the crazy thoughts I was having after my daughter got out of the hospital. It was embarrassing and illogical. I tried to get my thoughts under control on my own. I'll bet you can guess how that worked out for me! We need each other. I confessed to some close friends and asked them to pray for me.

They reminded me of truth but also gave me so much grace to struggle. They didn't shame me; they helped.

Our enemies are not Amalekites, but our flesh and the devil are at war with our spirits. We can't fight these enemies alone. At times we all need someone to hold up our arms with encouragement, prayer, and wisdom.

Is there someone in your sphere of influence right now who is going through a difficult time? Write below one practical way you can support that person in the coming week:

At times we are the ones needing others to hold us up, and other times we are the ones providing the support. We have different roles to play depending on God's directions in our lives. I love the picture in Exodus 17 of two necessary postures in battle. While Moses and his friends held the banner, the rest of the army was fighting. We need both elements to gain victory during difficult times. For example, we might pray about a job but never send out resumes or look for new opportunities. On the flip side, we might get so busy with the activity of trying to solve our problem that we forget to listen to the Lord. Supernatural options might be missed if we are too focused on the human side of things. We see a unique picture of the importance of prayer and action working together in the very first battle Israel faced in the wilderness. It wouldn't be their last, but they found victory through supernatural dependence and action on the field.

Take a moment to review our three key concepts from today's lesson and star the one that resonates most in your life today:

We need to raise a banner during weak moments.

We can't win our battles alone.

Prayer and action are necessary to win our battles.

A banner can help us remember the truth about God when we are struggling. When we want to quit, we can look to Jesus Christ. The prophet Jeremiah referred to Christ as the Righteous branch (Jeremiah 23:5). He is the banner that shows us how greatly God loves us, and the cross is the symbol of His sacrificial death for us. Through Jesus we have power to fight *every* battle.

Behold

Yahweh Nissi's name reminds us that when we are weary, we can focus on the amazing things God has done in the past to give us strength in the present and in the future.

Believe

Write a statement of belief:

Because you are Yahweh Nissi, I can _____.

Bloom

As you reflect on all you've learned about Yahweh Nissi today, ask the Lord to reveal any blind spots you may have when it comes to your current battles. Consider these questions, and then write any notes below:

- Have you been striving against people when the battle is not against flesh and blood (Ephesians 6:12)?
- What are some new ways you can approach your weak moments?
- Who might you pursue for a deeper relationship in order to help each other overcome current challenges?
- Where might you be out of balance when it comes to prayer and action?

Notes:

Yahweh Nissi is our banner. When we keep our eyes on Him, we can overcome even if we have failed in the past by a lack of faith or complaining. The Israelites didn't always get it right, but Yahweh was faithful to keep revealing more of Himself. As we look at more Yahweh compound names next week, we'll continue to grow a bigger view of God so that we can know Him more!

Talk with God

Yahweh Nissi, help me to remember often how You have worked in the past so I can trust You in the present! Show me what it would like to raise a banner today remembering all that You have done in my life. Reveal to me those alongside me who need strength and support today. I want to point them to You and support them as they seek You. Give me wisdom also to know how prayer and action are needed in my weary seasons. Amen.

Memory Verse Exercise

Read the Memory Verse on page 76 several times, and then fill in the blanks on the following page as you recite it:

_____ also _____ to _____, "_____ _____ __ the _____
of _____: _____, the _____ of _____ _____—
the _____ of _____, the _____ of _____, and the _____
of _____—has _____ ___ to _____.

_____ is my _____ _____,
    my _____ to _____ for all
        _____."

(Exodus 3:15)

Big Idea

Yahweh Nissi's name reminds us that when we are weary, we can focus on the amazing things God has done in the past to give us strength in the present.

Weekly Wrap Up

Review the Big Idea for each day, and then write any personal application that comes to mind.

Day 1: Yahweh Elohim—Unchanging God
Big Idea: Yahweh never changes, and the name Yahweh Elohim highlights God's personal relationship with us.

Personal Application:_____

_____

Day 2: Yahweh—The Self Existent One
Big Idea: Yahweh needs nothing from an outside source and has no beginning or end.

Personal Application:_____

_____

Day 3: Yahweh Yireh—The Lord Will Provide
Big Idea: Yahweh Yireh sees our needs and provides resources, people, and information according to His timetable for our ultimate good rather than our immediate pleasure.

Personal Application:_____

_____

Day 4: Yahweh Rapha—The Lord Who Heals You
Big Idea: Yahweh Rapha longs for each of us to experience ultimate
       healing.

Personal Application:_____

_____

Day 5: Yahweh Nissi—The Lord Our Banner
Big Idea: Yahweh Nissi's name reminds us that when we are weary, we
       can focus on the amazing things God has done in the past to
       give us strength in the present.

Personal Application:_____

_____

Video Viewer Guide: Week 3

When we are weary, we can focus on the amazing things God has done in the

_____ to give us strength in the _____.

Exodus 17:8-11

Deuteronomy 25:17-18

Victory is _____.

Victory requires _____.

Victory recognizes _____.

Exodus 17:12-15

1 Corinthians 10:3-4

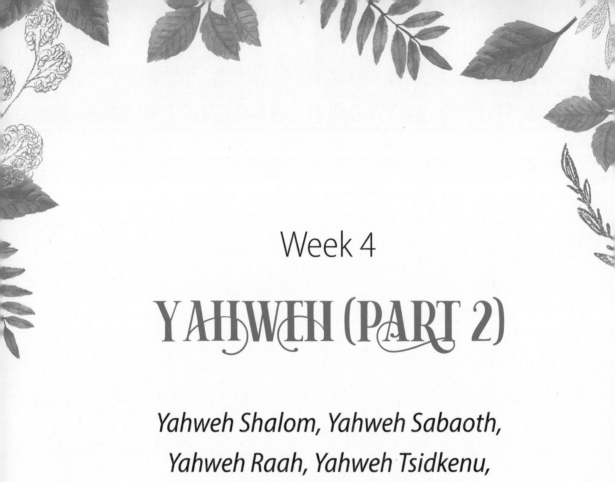

Week 4

YAHWEH (PART 2)

Yahweh Shalom, Yahweh Sabaoth,
Yahweh Raah, Yahweh Tsidkenu,
Yahweh Shammah

Memory Verse

Your name, O Lord, endures forever;
your fame, O Lord, is known to every generation.
(Psalm 135:13)

Day 1: Yahweh Shalom—The Lord Is Peace

Scripture Focus

Judges 6

So far in our study of God's names, we've found that God often reveals Himself to us in our places of *need*. When we need provision or healing, God says I am Yahweh Yireh or Yahweh Rapha.

As you think about what is needed in the world today, what are the first things that come to mind?

I can't help thinking of the beauty pageant cliché answer of "world peace." One of the reasons we need peace is that we are so stressed out. The American Psychological Institute reports that 77 percent of Americans say that they regularly experience physical symptoms from stress.[1] The top four symptoms they reported were fatigue, headache, upset stomach, and muscle tension. Psychological symptoms of stress were also reported, including feeling irritable, angry, nervous, tired (lack of energy), and as though you could cry.

What is causing stress in your life lately, whether something small or a major stressor?

We all lack peace from time to time. Fear and worry can creep in when we least expect them, leaving us awake at night. Maybe we think peace will descend upon us once our relational problems or financial worries are resolved. Other times we may think peace will come through having the right leaders in our government, job, or church. Our culture often hints that we need to create peace in our lives with a better time-management plan, more self-esteem, or an escape to a tropical island.

Today we will study God's name Yahweh Shalom, which means, "The Lord Is Peace." Together we will uncover this truth: *We don't create peace; we receive it from God.*

We can't engineer peace through work, play, or even rest. Instead, we receive it by trusting God and choosing to focus our thoughts on Him (Isaiah 26:3). True peace can be found only through a relationship with God. The Hebrew word *Shalom* means "completeness," "safety, soundness," "welfare," or "peace."[2] Yahweh is the Self-Existent One whose name is I AM. Through this name He is saying:

I AM peace.

This peace isn't a quick fix to temporal problems but a wholeness of mind, body, and soul in the midst of challenges.

While peace is a pervasive topic in Scripture, the name Yahweh Shalom appears only once, and we find this mention in the Book of Judges. God revealed Himself as peace to a man named Gideon during the time of the judges. Let's do a brief review of biblical history to see where the judges fit in the biblical time line.

During the period of the judges, the people of Israel lived in the Promised Land. Rather than discovering a utopian society there, they found that even in Canaan they faced opposition from enemies. They also drifted away from their relationship with Yahweh and adopted the gods of the surrounding nations. A cycle began to emerge. The people would sin, which led to them being conquered by other nations. Then they would cry out to the Lord to save them, and He would raise up a judge. That judge would help deliver the people from their enemies, and Israel would serve the Lord. Over time, they would again drift into the sin of idolatry and the cycle would repeat itself.

Creation and the Fall

Noah and the Flood

God promises Abraham many descendants

Jacob wrestles with God and becomes Israel

400 years of slavery in Egypt

Moses leads the people out of Egypt

40 years of wilderness wandering

Joshua leads Israel into the Promised Land

God raises up judges

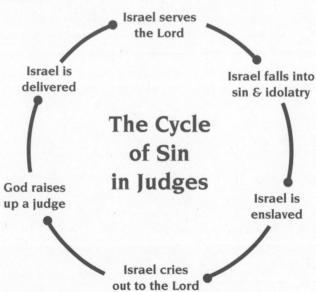

The Cycle of Sin in Judges

Israel serves the Lord

Israel falls into sin & idolatry

Israel is delivered

God raises up a judge

Israel is enslaved

Israel cries out to the Lord

When the Israelites turned away from God, their enemies defeated them. Their disobedience left them vulnerable without supernatural help.

Read Judges 6:1-16 and fill in the blanks:

The Israelites did _____ in Yahweh's sight, so they were oppressed by Midian for _____ years. (v. 1)

The Midianites treated the people of Israel _____. (vv. 2-5, answers will vary)

After Israel was reduced to starvation, they cried out to _____ for help. (v. 6)

God reminded the people through a prophet that He was Yahweh Elohim but accused the people of _____. (v. 10)

The angel of the Lord found a man named _____ threshing wheat at the bottom of a winepress. (v. 11)

The angel said to Gideon, "_____ _____." (v. 12)

Gideon questioned the angel because of all the hardships his people endured and claimed that Yahweh had _____ them. (v. 13)

The Lord then spoke to Gideon telling him to go rescue Israel with _____. (v. 14)

Gideon questioned God's directive because his clan was the weakest and he was the _____ in his family. (v. 15)

God assured Gideon that He would _____. (v. 16)

Here we find the Israelites robbed of peace as they live in fear for their lives and their livelihoods. God appeared to Gideon with a message of hope, but Gideon asked God for a sign of confirmation. The angel patiently waited as Gideon went home and cooked a goat and baked bread. Then Gideon returned with a basket of meat and a pot of broth and presented them to the angel. When the angel touched his staff to the food, it was consumed with flames. Afterward, the angel disappeared.

Extra Insight

The Moabites came from the line of Lot, Abraham's nephew, while the Midianites were descendants of Abraham and Hagar's son, Ishmael. Moses's wife, Zipporah, was a Midianite. When the Midianites aligned themselves with the Moabites, they became enemies of Israel.

Read Judges 6:22-24 and summarize what happened next:

Gideon feared God more than the Midianites once He was certain that it was really God speaking to him. I've had many times when I wasn't sure whether God was calling me to do something or it was my own imagination. Once Gideon saw the food turn to dust, he took a humble posture. God didn't shame him for needing some confirmation.

Many English versions translate the beginning of Judges 6:23 with the word *peace*.

> *"Peace be to you."* (ESV)
> *"Peace!"* (NIV)
> *"Peace be unto thee."* (KJV)
> *"Peace to you."* (NASB)

The New Living Translation puts it this way: "It is all right." God reminded Gideon that not only was He *with* Gideon, He was *for* him. Yahweh Shalom wants us to know that as well. He is not just *with* us, He is *for* us. *Shalom* isn't something we create. We receive it by faith when we believe that God says it will be all right.

Let's define what it means for "peace to be with us" or that "it will be all right." Here's what God didn't say:

- You will never be scared again. (Gideon shows fear in Judges 6:27.)
- You will never need more confirmation. (Gideon asks for another sign in chapter 7.)
- Everything will make sense. (Yahweh asks Gideon to reduce his army from thirty-two thousand to three hundred.)
- You won't have battles. (Gideon later fights the Midianites.)

Peace isn't tied to circumstances. Gideon faced personal, family, and national distress. He encountered Yahweh Shalom in the middle of his stressors and declared that God was Yahweh Shalom *before* he experienced relief from the oppression of his enemies.

As you reflect on Gideon's story from Judges 6, what principles about peace stand out to you?

You may have different insights, but these stood out to me:

- Sin steals our peace.
- The road to peace is the road back to God.
- Peace can be a side effect of obedience.
- Sometimes we don't realize that God is all we need until He is all we have.

When life feels stressful, I usually try to fix things. I want those I love to feel happy and often tie my own peace to that outcome. But there is a difference between happiness and peace. Happiness is connected to what happens; peace is a state of the heart and mind. We can't conjure up peace, but that doesn't stop us from trying.

Here are some questions to consider. Jot some responses below if anything comes to mind.

- **Is there sin in your life that might be stealing your peace?**
- **What might the road back to God look like for you?**
- **How have you experienced the side effect of peace when you have walked in obedience to God?**

When you feel stress, where do you usually turn for relief?

When I was a young mom, I would have answered that question with "hiding in the bathroom." Right now my go-to reactions to stress usually center around these three things:

- Productivity—Getting things accomplished brings a sense of order out of chaos.
- Distraction—Social media, online games, or television provides a temporary escape.
- Problem solving—Brainstorming and implementing some kind of solution in an attempt to stop the stressful situation helps reduce my anxiety.

These things might seem to relieve our stress, but they can only bring temporary reprieve. Yahweh Shalom offers us true peace that embodies health

Extra Insight

While Yahweh Shalom's name is found only in the Book of Judges, we know that Isaiah identified the Messiah as the Prince of Peace (Isaiah 9:6).

"I am leaving you with a gift—peace of mind and heart. And the peace I give is a gift the world cannot give. So don't be troubled or afraid."

(John 14:27)

and wholeness. This *shalom* can fill us with an inner calm even when problems abound.

> **Read John 14:27 and John 16:33 in the margin. What do these verses tell us about the gift of peace?**

"I have told you all this so that you may have peace in me. Here on earth you will have many trials and sorrows. But take heart, because I have overcome the world."

(John 16:33)

Jesus knows our tendency toward fear, worry, and stress, and He wants to calm our hearts and minds. He says that if we put our trust in Him, it will be all right.

Behold

God is Yahweh Shalom, The Lord Is Peace.

Believe

Write a statement of belief:

Because Yahweh Shalom is the God of peace, I can _____

_____ **in the midst of today's stressors.**

Bloom

Talking about peace is one thing; practically receiving it from God when we experience stress is another. Isaiah 26:3 says, "You will keep in perfect peace all who trust in you, all whose thoughts are fixed on you!" Instead of trying to fix our circumstances, we should fix our minds on God; that can help us to receive the peace of God when life feels out of control.

Take a moment to think about the names of God we've already studied. Pick a few that come to mind and write them below. (If you have trouble recalling them, turn to page 204 for a list of all the names and their meanings.) Then spend a few moments fixing your thoughts on God and the character qualities these names reveal about Him:

Name of God **Meaning of Name**

I pray that focusing on God's names and character will bring a peaceful perspective to whatever is on your plate today!

Talk with God

Lord, I want to remember that You are Yahweh Shalom. Help me to stop trying to create peace in my life and instead run to You to receive it. You know all the things that are stressing me out, Lord. Sometimes it seems overwhelming. Help me to trust You more so that I will obey You more. I don't want to drift away from You as the Israelites did during the time of the judges. I believe that when I seek You, it will be all right. Amen.

Memory Verse Exercise

Read the Memory Verse on page 108 several times, and then fill in the blanks below as you recite it:

Your _____, O Lᴏʀᴅ, endures forever;

> *your _____, O Lᴏʀᴅ, is known to every generation.*

(Psalm 135:13)

Day 2: Yahweh Sabaoth— The Lord of Heaven's Armies

Big Idea

We don't create peace; we receive it from Yahweh Shalom.

I remember my thoughts and emotions swirling with questions. Friendships that I treasured were falling apart. No matter how many meetings and conversations we had, reconciliation wasn't happening. I prayed in anguish, asking God to help me see clearly. It wasn't a physical war, but every day felt like an inner battle during that season. I needed to respond to the hurtful words and actions of others. Knowing when to initiate and engage and when to pull back and stay silent was a significant part of the process. I needed God to deliver me from the internal battle in my thoughts and emotions, as well as the external battle of conflict. When have you found yourself in some kind of "battle" in *your* life?

Today we will discover that God revealed Himself in Scripture as Yahweh Sabaoth, the Lord of Heaven's Armies. He is our strength in life's battles. Thankfully, not every season carries the intensity of battle. Like the weather, we often experience sunshine after a storm.

Scripture Focus

1 Samuel 1:1-18; 17:45-47

As you think about your current circumstances, circle the weather icon below that most closely describes them:

Sunny   Partly Sunny   Partly Cloudy   Cloudy   Rain   Thunderstorms

Whether you are in a sunny or stormy season, we know that life can change like the weather. Challenges can surface slowly or suddenly.

Hannah was a woman in the Bible who knew a little something about storms. She was unable to have children during a time in history when women were defined by their ability to bear sons. We find her story in 1 Samuel during the end of the period of the judges.

Read 1 Samuel 1:1-18 and answer the following questions:

What additional problem did Hannah experience because of her infertility? (v. 6)

Who tried to comfort her? (v. 8)

Where did Hannah take her problems? (v. 9)

What name for God is used in verses 3 and 11?

Depending on your translation, you likely found the first mention of Yahweh Sabaoth using one of these phrases:

Extra Insight

Devout Israelite parents were expected to commit their firstborn son to the Lord, a requirement of the Mosaic Law. Hannah went a step further and dedicated the entire life of her anticipated son for service to the Lord likely as a Nazirite.[5]

- Lord of hosts (ESV, NASB, KJV)
- Lord Almighty (NIV)
- Lord of Heaven's Armies (NLT)

The Hebrew term is *Yahweh Tsaba*, which often was translated into the Greek term "Lord Sabaoth." *Tsaba* means "that which goes forth, army, war, warfare, host."[3] Hannah found herself in a battle as she struggled against Peninnah. In verse 6, when it records that Peninnah taunted and made fun of Hannah, we find the Hebrew word *ra'am*, which means "to thunder."[4] Peninnah thundered at Hannah, intensifying the storm that already raged in her heart because of her infertility.

Hannah's battle wasn't against advancing armies but took place in her heart and home. She went alone to the Tabernacle and pleaded her case with the Lord of Heaven's Armies. Yahweh Sabaoth commands the angels and holds the stars in His hands. Hannah poured out her heart and believed by faith that she had been heard.

What challenging situations have you been facing lately?

What did you notice that Hannah did not do in reacting to Peninnah?

Identify some different ways that people react when another person intensifies their pain:

We don't have any record of Hannah retorting with an insult or fighting back. She could have told Peninnah that Elkanah loved her more or criticized Peninnah's parenting. When someone hurts us, often our natural inclination is to hurt back. Instead, Hannah ran to the Lord. She prayed with such emotion that Eli thought she was drunk!

As you think about any storms in your life recently or in the past, how have you responded?

At times we lash back at frustrating people, and other times we run to the Lord.

Read Ephesians 6:11-12 in the margin and summarize their message below:

How do these verses affirm Hannah's actions?

The Peninnahs in our lives are not our real enemies. Yahweh Sabaoth reminds us that He commands an army of angels that are fighting unseen but very real enemies. As we consider what this means for us in our day-to-day lives, we find that praying to Yahweh Sabaoth is our best spiritual battle tactic.

[11]*Put on all of God's armor so that you will be able to stand firm against all strategies of the devil.* [12]*For we are not fighting against flesh-and-blood enemies, but against evil rulers and authorities of the unseen world, against mighty powers in this dark world, and against evil spirits in the heavenly places.*
(Ephesians 6:11-12)

Read Ephesians 6:13-18 below and circle each piece of armor:

¹³**Therefore, put on every piece of God's armor so you will be able to resist the enemy in the time of evil. Then after the battle you will still be standing firm.** ¹⁴**Stand your ground, putting on the belt of truth and the body armor of God's righteousness.** ¹⁵**For shoes, put on the peace that comes from the Good News so that you will be fully prepared.** ¹⁶**In addition to all of these, hold up the shield of faith to stop the fiery arrows of the devil.** ¹⁷**Put on salvation as your helmet, and take the sword of the Spirit, which is the word of God.**

¹⁸**Pray in the Spirit at all times and on every occasion. Stay alert and be persistent in your prayers for all believers everywhere.**

As we pray, we can specifically ask God for the armor—the belt of truth, the body armor (breastplate) of righteousness, the shoes of peace, the shield of faith, the helmet of salvation, the sword of the Spirit, which is the Word of God. We acknowledged at the beginning of today's lesson that we all go through seasons, so I want to give us two options as we put feet to Hannah's story. Hannah prayed about her situation, and we can too!

Read the options below and choose the one that best connects with your current circumstances:

Option #1: If you are in a stormy situation—whether it be with people, finances, health, emotions, or some other difficulty—write a prayer to Yahweh Sabaoth. Pray for God's armor to protect you, and ask for His deliverance. Write your prayer below:

Option #2: We don't always have a specific battle because, mercifully, we encounter sunny seasons. Take a moment to praise God for peaceful circumstances, and then think about the people in your life. Are any of them in the midst of a storm? Would you pray to the Lord of Heaven's Armies on their behalf right now? Pray specific pieces of the armor over them, writing your prayer below:

Recently a coworker of mine lost her best friend in a car crash. I was traveling with my coworker the day she got the news that her twenty-six-year-old best friend had died. I felt at such a loss to comfort her knowing that I couldn't soothe her pain. So instead I prayed to the One I know can. Running to Yahweh Sabaoth in prayer is our best spiritual battle tactic. God answered Hannah's prayer, and she had a son named Samuel. This boy would eventually be a great leader who anointed kings in Israel. One of these future kings was named David.

While still in his youth, David went into the Israelite army camp to bring some food to his brothers. When he saw a giant taunting the people of Israel, he took action. Whereas Hannah was responding to internal trials, David initiated a very physical battle. This boy called on the same God for help—Yahweh Sabaoth.

Read 1 Samuel 17:45-47 and then answer the following questions.

Describe the confidence that David had in Yahweh Sabaoth.

Read 1 Samuel 17:48-51, and summarize the ending below:

No one had been willing to fight the Philistine giant because of his size and strength. David gathered five stones and killed the giant with a rock flung from a slingshot in just the right spot. He trusted the Lord to guide his hands and win his battle. David initiated and participated with full confidence in the power of His God. He knew that Yahweh Sabaoth commanded an army of angels and made the sun, moon, and stars.

Sometimes the size and strength of our challenging circumstances can feel overwhelming. When we work through the logic and emotion, we don't see how we can overcome our obstacles. It's helpful to remember that often it's a process that takes time. As I battled my feelings and frustrations in friendships, everything didn't work out overnight. Some battles are long and may not ever be fully reconciled. However, even though every relationship may not heal, our hearts always can. Our circumstances may or may not change, but our perspective always will when we take a posture of faith. Like Hannah and David, we can grow a bigger view of God as we behold Yahweh Sabaoth, the Lord of Heaven's Armies.

Behold

> The LORD of Heaven's Armies is here among us;
>   the God of Israel is our fortress.
>   (Psalm 46:7)

Extra Insight

Yahweh Sabaoth is the most frequent compound title for God used in the Old Testament, appearing over 240 times.[6]

Believe

Write a statement of belief:

Yahweh Sabaoth is _____ and He is able

to _____ in my life today.

Bloom

As you think about all you have learned about Yahweh Sabaoth today, write some reflections below about who He is and how it affects the way you think about your battles:

Yahweh Sabaoth delivered Hannah from her shame and David from a giant. He provides His armor of protection for us as we fight our battles. He may not always fix our circumstances, but He always will change our outlook as we witness His power and authority as the Lord of Heaven's Armies.

Talk with God

Yahweh Sabaoth, You are the Lord over the angels. Your power is greater than my mind can conceive. I am asking You to buckle the belt of truth around my waist. Protect my heart today with Your breastplate of righteousness. Help me to lace up the shoes of peace so that everywhere I walk, Your good news of peace will tread. I'm holding up the shield of faith. As I believe the things I can't see, I pray You will increase my faith to put out the fiery arrows of doubt that come at me. Lord, place the helmet of salvation on my head. Help me fix my mind on You and take every runaway thought captive. I thank You for being the living Word. Protect me with Your armor and deliver me today. Amen.

Big Idea

We can find strength in life's battles as we trust Yahweh Sabaoth, the Lord of Heaven's Armies.

Memory Verse Exercise

Read the Memory Verse on page 108 several times, and then fill in the blanks below as you recite it:

Your _____, O _____, endures forever;

    your _____, O _____, is known to every generation.

                                    (Psalm 135:13)

Day 3: Yahweh Raah— The Lord My Shepherd

Scripture Focus

Psalm 23

I haven't spent much time with sheep, and I can honestly say I have never met a shepherd. The barnyard petting area at the local zoo where I took my kids when they were little is the extent of my experience with sheep. What about you?

What is the first thing that comes to your mind when you think of sheep?

Maybe you count them at night to fall asleep or have memories of county fairs. The reason we are talking sheep today is that one of the names for God is Yahweh Raah, the Lord My Shepherd. Because of the agrarian society of the original audience of the Scriptures, we find many references to sheep. Here are a few examples:

> Acknowledge that the LORD is God!
> > He made us, and we are his.
> > We are his people, the sheep of his pasture.
> > > (Psalm 100:3)

> All of us, like sheep, have strayed away.
> > We have left God's paths to follow our own.
> Yet the LORD laid on him
> > the sins of us all.
> > > (Isaiah 53:6)

> "I am the good shepherd; I know my own sheep, and they know me, just as my Father knows me and I know the Father. So I sacrifice my life for the sheep."
> > (John 10:14-15)

Extra Insight

Jesus identified Himself as that expected "good shepherd" (John 10:14), but He is also called the "great Shepherd" (Hebrews 13:20) and "the Chief Shepherd" (1 Peter 5:4).[7]

God wanted His people to know Him, so He used illustrations they could connect with their real lives. One of the most famous passages of Scripture regarding sheep was written by King David, who had been a shepherd in his boyhood. He understood the importance of a shepherd knowing that sheep require more attention and care than any other class of livestock.[8]

Although I've had very little interaction with sheep and shepherds personally, I gained some insights into God's name as Yahweh Raah from reading a book written by a shepherd. In his book A Shepherd Looks at Psalm 23,

W. Phillip Keller uses his personal experience to make connections between his work as a shepherd and spiritual life. I will be referencing some of his insights to help us get a clearer picture of God's character as a shepherd in our lives.

Before we get started, do you know any characteristics of sheep that might help us understand why Scripture sometimes compares people to them? If so, note them below:

Some characteristics of sheep that might help clarify why Scripture compares them to people include

- a mob instinct, fears, timidity, stubbornness, and stupidity;[9]
- a tendency to be gentle, obedient, and quiet.

Even though we sometimes display a sheep's less desirable qualities, God chooses us, calls us by name, and takes care of us. Shepherds name and put their identifying mark on their sheep. Some shepherds take excellent care of their sheep, while others neglect them. Keller says it this way, "The Master in people's lives makes the difference in their destiny."[10]

Read Psalm 23 and list some of the benefits you find for those who have Yahweh Raah as their master:

How have you personally experienced at least one of these benefits in your life?

This psalm lists many blessings for those who have made Yahweh Raah their master, but we will focus on only four today:

- contentment,
- restoration,

- guidance, and
- protection.

Contentment

David writes that when the Lord is our shepherd, we have all that we need (Psalm 23:1). We can rest in green pastures beside quiet waters (Psalm 23:2). To lie down a sheep must be free of fear, tension, aggravations, and hunger.[11] Sheep face all sorts of predators. Keller tells of losing sheep to attacks from dogs and cougars. When he slept in the field or came quickly from his bed at the sound of any disturbance, the sheep's fears were calmed. He writes, "Nothing so quieted and reassured the sheep as to see me in the field."[12]

While dogs and coyotes are not often what produce our fears, we know what it's like to be scared. We live in a world full of dangers. Jobs are lost, people die, accidents happen, and relationships end. At times we can be paralyzed by what might happen. But when we know that our Good Shepherd is watching over us, we can rest.

Another contentment inhibitor for sheep is tension. Just like humans, sheep can develop pecking orders and disturb one another. They have foolish rivalries among themselves. When the shepherd appears, they forget these silly comparisons and turn their attention to him. Likewise, we can turn to God and find rest for the tensions in our churches, families, and communities.

Aggravations like flies and ticks also prevent sheep from lying down to rest.[13] A good shepherd applies repellents. This takes time and extra care as the shepherd watches them for signs and applies oil to their heads. Perhaps you can relate to having irritations that have been bugging you and keeping you from God's rest. The Good Shepherd is the place to turn when we find ourselves in this predicament.

Hunger also prohibits a sheep from being able to rest. Most pasturelands are arid and dry places. The shepherd works to clear rocks and dead foliage and pasture their sheep near water. Our good shepherd also wants us to have good spiritual food and water so that we can rest in Him.

As you think about the four rest-inhibitors for sheep, put a check mark beside the one(s) that is/are interfering with your rest lately:

_____ fear   _____ tension   _____ aggravations   _____ hunger

Here are some practical ways God might be calling you to trust Him more as your Good Shepherd:

- When we bring our fears to God instead of dwelling on them, we are trusting the Good Shepherd.
- When we stop comparing ourselves with others and keep our eyes on the Lord, we are trusting the Good Shepherd.

- When we bring our irritations to God instead of throwing a fit about them, we are trusting the Good Shepherd.
- When we ask the Lord to give us an appetite for spiritual things rather than worldly pleasures, we are trusting the Good Shepherd.

Are there any you would add to this list? If so, write them below:

Contentment is a great blessing for those who have made Yahweh Raah their master.

Restoration

Depending on your translation, Psalm 23:3 says that Yahweh Raah "restores my soul" (ESV, NKJV, NASB), "refreshes my soul" (NIV), or "renews my strength." As a shepherd, Keller believes this refers to a "cast down" sheep. He writes, "This is an old English shepherd's term for a sheep that has turned over on its back and cannot get up again by itself."[14] Sheep in the cast-down position have become stuck upside down from either being overconfident in where they stepped, lazy in resting and rolling, or being too fat to carry themselves. The shepherd rolls the sheep over and rubs the extremities to encourage circulation. Then he or she can help them stand again. This is a personal process between sheep and shepherd when a sheep has gotten itself into a dangerous position.

This reminds us that God longs to rescue us when we've gotten ourselves into trouble. Jesus tells a story about a lost sheep in Luke 15. He says that the shepherd will leave the ninety-nine to go after the one who is lost. Even if the sheep is cast down because of his own bad decision, Jesus pursues and restores.

Have you experienced God's restoration when you've felt like that upside-down sheep in your life? If the Lord has lovingly met you in a time when you were struggling, record it here:

Guidance

Sheep need guidance because, left to their own devices, they will gnaw a pasture all the way to the roots and destroy the grass. They also will spend too much time in a favored spot and wear it down so that the ground is more susceptible to parasites. Keller says that the best safeguard for a shepherd is to keep his flock on the move![15]

Psalm 23 assures us that Yahweh Raah will guide us on right paths to honor His name (Psalm 23:3). Sometimes those right paths lead us through a dark valley. Keller points out that the valleys often have water sources and rich feed and foliage. When given the choice, we probably wouldn't pick dark valleys as an option to travel, but we can follow our Shepherd knowing His paths are best.

I had the opportunity to pray on the phone today with a friend who needed guidance. I wish I could have told her what she should do, but I had no idea! Both options seemed difficult to me. It was no accident that today I was studying Yahweh Raah, the Good Shepherd who guides us. I prayed for her. I cried out to Yahweh Raah to show her which path to take. We often are like sheep. We don't like change and tend to wear the grass down in the same spot. Our Shepherd needs to move us along, and He shows us right paths.

Is there an area where you need guidance today? Perhaps you or a loved one needs to know what next steps to follow. Take a moment to write a few sentences in prayer to Yahweh Raah, asking for specific direction either for you or the someone in your life:

Protection

A shepherd doesn't have a large suitcase. They travel light, but each one carries a rod and a staff. The rod is a weapon of authority, defense, and discipline. The shepherd might use it to correct a sheep that is going off course or to fight off a predator.[16] The staff is a rounded-looking stick that identifies a shepherd as a shepherd. We used plastic ones for the shepherds in the Christmas pageant so the audience could discern their characters from Joseph or the wise men. The staff could be used to lift a newborn lamb to its mother or draw a sheep close for examination.

As our Good Shepherd, the Lord will defend us from external enemies but also protect us from our own tendency to stray. His rod of protection and staff of compassion are meant to comfort us.

Yahweh Raah wants to lovingly shepherd us. He offers us:

- contentment,
- restoration,
- guidance, and
- protection.

Of these four shepherding qualities, which one most resonates with you today?

As you think about your role as a sheep, are there any steps you could take to cooperate more fully with the care that Yahweh Raah offers you?

Jesus told us that He is the Good Shepherd who sacrifices His life for the sheep (John 10:15). When we behold and believe more fully the truths of Yahweh Raah, we can bloom with contentment, restoration, guidance, and protection!

Behold

Yahweh Raah lovingly cares for His sheep.

Believe

Write a statement of belief:

Because I know that Yahweh Raah is _____,

I can _____.

Bloom

As you reflect on today's study of Yahweh Raah, what stands out to you?

My prayer for each of us is that we would know God more. When we really believe that He is the source of our contentment, restoration, guidance, and protection, we can worry less and trust more.

Talk with God

Yahweh Raah, You are my master. Show me where to rest. I want to trust You with my fears, tensions, aggravations, and appetites. You are the One who picks me up when I fall over. Restore me so that I can follow You. Lord, I need Your guidance. Show me which paths to choose. Thank You for protecting me. Help me to trust Your rod of correction and Your staff of compassion. Life can feel scary, but I know I am safe with You. Amen.

Memory Verse Exercise

Read the Memory Verse on page 108 several times, and then fill in the blanks on the following page as you recite it:

Big Idea

Yahweh Raah wants to lovingly shepherd His people and offers contentment, restoration, guidance, and protection.

Your _____, O _____, _____ forever;
      your _____, O _____, is _____ to every generation.

(Psalm 135:13)

Day 4: Yahweh Tsidkenu— The Lord Is Our Righteousness

When our children were young, we made a family covenant with standards about when our kids could date or get their ears pierced. We don't think every family should have the same rules. My husband lovingly refers to them as our "personal legalisms." Our college kids still bemoan that our family rules include no tattoos or extra piercings until they are financially independent. I don't think it's the "right" way for every family, but it's the standard we've chosen for ours.

In our covenant, my husband and I decided our personal family standards. Many gray areas exist in parenting and culture. We must delineate between moral absolutes and applying wisdom. When it comes to morality, some standards apply to all people, which means they can't be right for one person and wrong for another.

What are some basic laws that our culture believes apply to all people?

Scripture Focus

Jeremiah 23:1-8

Most people would agree that it is wrong to harm children, murder, lie, rape, or steal. When it comes to following God, we don't use our logic or emotions to decide what is right or wrong. God sets the standard of righteousness. He gave instructions through laws, prophets, and His inspired Scriptures. While we must correctly interpret the Bible and apply it to our modern-day situations, we don't get to pick and choose which of God's standards we feel like following.

Because the original audience of the Bible lived in a culture much different from our own, we are tasked with unwrapping culture to lift up the principles and apply them in our own contexts. The Old Testament gives us great insight into the New Covenant, but we are not bound by many laws regarding diet, molds, or rules that applied to a particular nation. We need wisdom in reading and applying Scripture, but we don't have to guess regarding Yahweh's opinions about murder, cheating, or the neglect of the poor. He gave us the Bible so that we have a clear sense of His boundaries.

Today we will uncover this truth: *God is righteousness, and He makes us righteous through Christ.*

We have been looking at the first mentions of each name in Scripture, and today we will encounter *Yahweh Tsidkenu*, the Lord Is Our Righteousness, in the writings of the prophet Jeremiah. Jeremiah referenced Christ over six hundred

Extra Insight

Tsidkenu is pronounced tsid-KAY-nu.[17]

years before Jesus's birth in Bethlehem. God's plan from the beginning was to restore our righteousness through His Son. Let's take a brief walk through biblical history after the period of the judges.

Because they wanted to mimic the surrounding nations, God's people asked for a human king to rule them. Hannah's son Samuel anointed both Saul and David as kings. David's son Solomon then ruled as the final monarch in the United Kingdom of Israel. Solomon's son Rehoboam couldn't hold on to the kingdom when an army commander named Jeroboam rebelled against him and took the ten northern tribes and formed a new nation. The period of the Divided Kingdom included Israel in the north, which was ruled by all wicked kings who did not follow Yahweh, and the Southern Kingdom of Judah, which had a few glimmers of revival but ultimately rebelled against God's standards.

The prophet Jeremiah spoke God's messages to the Southern Kingdom of Judah during the forty years before they went into exile because of their disobedience. Instead of adhering to God's covenants with them, they adopted the practices of the surrounding nations including idolatry, greed, and immorality. They failed to listen to Yahweh's words and hardened their hearts against Him. During this season of rebellion, God revealed the compound name *Yahweh Tsidkenu*. This name comes from the Hebrew word *tsedeq*, which means "justice, rightness, righteousness."[18]

While *tsedeq* is used over one hundred times in the Old Testament, it is only paired with Yahweh, the Self-Existent One, two times. Both of these are found in Jeremiah's writings.

> **Read Jeremiah 23:1-8 and draw a line to match the person(s) with their description:**

Person

1. **Shepherds of the Sheep (Leaders of God's people)**

2. **The Lord Is Our Righteousness**

3. **King David**

4. **Sheep (people of Israel and Judah)**

Description

a. **righteous descendant who will rule with wisdom and do what is just and right**

b. **This remnant will be gathered back from the countries where they have been scattered. God will appoint responsible shepherds to care for them.**

c. **Leaders who have destroyed and scattered the people they should have cared for.**

d. **The Lord Our Righteousness would come through this royal leader's lineage**

One theme we find throughout Scripture is that like sheep, God's people are prone to wander off the path of righteousness. We can't manufacture our own right living. Through Jeremiah's words, God provided hope for the future, promising that He would raise up the antidote for our unrighteousness. Right living isn't just about our outward actions; it is a condition of the heart. It was Jeremiah who exposed the human condition apart from God. He said, "The human heart is the most deceitful of all things, and desperately wicked. Who really knows how bad it is?" (Jeremiah 17:9). When it comes to right living, we don't need behavior modification; we need heart transformation.

This is what the Lord promised through Yahweh Tsidkenu. The prophet Ezekiel wrote his messages at the same time as Jeremiah, and he referenced the heart when he spoke about the future Messianic days.

Read Ezekiel 36:26-27 in the margin. How do these verses support the idea of right living as internal exchange rather than external behavior change?

How did Christ fulfill the Scriptures we've read in Jeremiah and Ezekiel?

Read Romans 3:21-22 and 2 Corinthians 5:21 in the margin. What additional insights do you gain from these verses regarding how Christ fulfilled Jeremiah's prophecy regarding Yahweh Tsidkenu?

Jesus became righteousness for us. God knew we couldn't manufacture it on our own. Positionally, Christ became the ultimate sacrifice to satisfy the payment for our unrighteousness.

Take a moment to pause and write a prayer of gratitude to Yahweh Tsidkenu for becoming righteousness for you:

Just as God makes us righteous, satisfying the penalty of sin through Christ, so His power enables us to live the Christian life through the Holy Spirit. Christ wants to conform us more and more into His image. Practically, we are still fighting the battle against the flesh, and surrendering to the Spirit in how we live

26*And I will give you a new heart, and I will put a new spirit in you. I will take out your stony, stubborn heart and give you a tender, responsive heart.* 27*And I will put my Spirit in you so that you will follow my decrees and be careful to obey my regulations.*
(Ezekiel 36:26-27)

21*But now God has shown us a way to be made right with him without keeping the requirements of the law, as was promised in the writings of Moses and the prophets long ago.* 22*We are made right with God by placing our faith in Jesus Christ. And this is true for everyone who believes, no matter who we are.*
(Romans 3:21-22)

For God made Christ, who never sinned, to be the offering for our sin, so that we could be made right with God through Christ.
(2 Corinthians 5:21)

righteous lives. Our culture blurs the lines of right and wrong, and we can easily follow the herd into compromising God's standards when we live according to the flesh and choose to do what feels good in the moment.

I struggle with this regularly. I know that Christ's righteousness is needed for my right standing with God. Yet I often try in my own strength to make right choices in the day-to-day decisions. I'm grateful for the apostle Paul's letter to the church in Galatia, in which he writes, "How foolish can you be? After starting your new lives in the Spirit, why are you now trying to become perfect by your own human effort?" (Galatians 3:3).

How can you relate to the tension between choosing human effort and yielding to divine power in your own practical pursuit of right living this week?

In my human effort I strive to pray and read my Bible. The impact of media and cultural messages can deaden my ability to uphold godly standards without me even realizing it. I seek to work at love, kindness, and patience when God has clearly told me these are the fruit of His Spirit at work in me (Galatians 5:22-23). Our part is to yield, and God's part is to work in us.

I wish I could write a five- or seven-step process for how to yield to the Holy Spirit instead of relying on human strength. Instead, I know it looks different for each person. It's a relationship rather than a step-by-step process—though spiritual practices can help us to practice yielding or surrendering to God's loving, faithful presence. The truth is that, for many of us it often looks like coming to the end of ourselves after we've exhausted our human efforts, saying, "I can't, but I believe you can, God." That's when the power of God's righteousness becomes more apparent in our lives.

However we come to the point of yielding to the Spirit, it is faith alone that activates the supernatural ability to make right choices. God's Spirit also helps us interpret and understand His authoritative Word. Unlike parenting standards that might vary from family to family, God's standards are not up for debate. My children may try to negotiate our family covenant, but we cannot change God's mind about how righteousness is defined. He Himself embodies justice and rightness, for He is Yahweh Tsidkenu, the Lord Is Our Righteousness. The good news is that He not only wants to be our righteousness but also to transform our hearts so that we become more like Him.

Behold

God is Yahweh Tsidkenu, the Lord Is Our Righteousness. He makes us righteous through Christ.

Believe

Write a statement of belief. (Remember, there is no right or wrong answer here!)

I believe you are Yahweh Tsidkenu, so I will stop _____

_____ and instead _____.

Bloom

While we can't create our own ability to live right, we can ask God to give us an appetite for right living. Jesus said, "Blessed are those who hunger and thirst for righteousness, for they will be filled" (Matthew 5:6 NIV). We can bloom in righteousness as we draw near to Yahweh Tsidkenu and ask Him to give us a hunger and thirst for Him.

Talk with God

Lord, You know the world around me tries to define what is right, but help me to hold fast to Your standards. You alone are truly righteous. Thank You for being my righteousness through the promised Messiah, Jesus Christ. Give me discernment to grow in a greater understanding of what is right and wrong according to Your Word, and teach me to surrender to Your Spirit moment by moment. Give me a greater desire to live in and through Your Spirit so that I may honor and glorify You. In Jesus's name. Amen.

Memory Verse Exercise

Read the Memory Verse on page 108 several times, and then fill in the blanks below as you recite it:

_____ _____, O _____, _____ *forever;*
_____ _____, O _____, *is* _____ *to every generation.*
(Psalm 135:13)

Big Idea

Yahweh Tsidkenu is righteousness, and He makes us righteous through Christ.

Day 5: Yahweh Shammah— The Lord Is There

The story is told of Reginald III, Duke of Guelders, who lived in what is now Belgium in the 1300s. When Reginald became the heir to the throne, his younger brother Edward led a revolt against him and had a special room built for him in a castle. He put no locks on the doors or windows. The door was big enough for a person of normal size and stature to exit, but Reginald was obese. He only needed to lose weight in order to leave his room. His brother knew his

Scripture Focus

Ezekiel 48

weakness for sweets and had a tray of delicacies delivered every day. Reginald became a prisoner of his appetite, only leaving the room when the walls were cut for his release after Edward's death.[19]

This story illustrates that we can become captives by our own design. God brought the nation of Israel out of slavery in Egypt and into the Promised Land after forty years in the wilderness. Yahweh gave them laws through His servant Moses and promised blessings in the land if they would honor His commands. After the period of the judges, the people of Israel were ruled by kings. They divided into two nations with Israel in the north being carried away into captivity in 722 BC by the nation of Assyria. The Southern Kingdom of Judah was on the brink of exile over one hundred years later because they had not learned from the demise of their northern neighbors. They also rebelled against the Lord by worshiping false gods and failing to obey Yahweh's instructions.

While Jeremiah was preaching a message of repentance in the land of Judah, another man was writing and speaking similar words to the exiles who had already been taken to Babylon. When King Nebuchadnezzar first invaded Judah, he took the best resources of the land and imposed a tax that had to be paid into his coffers. On a second visit to Judah, Nebuchadnezzar took more people and resettled them in Babylon. Ezekiel was taken on this second visit and spoke the same message to Jewish Babylonian exiles that Jeremiah was giving to those still living in Judah.

Today in Ezekiel's writings we will discover the name Yahweh Shammah, The Lord Is There.

What comes to your mind as you hear this name for God?

I asked my teenage daughter what she thought it meant that one of God's names is "The Lord Is There." She said she took it to mean that God is here, there, and everywhere. There certainly is truth in that observation. As we dig into Ezekiel's book, we will find context that provides even greater insight into this name through a story about captives. Our main focus today will be this truth of Yahweh Shammah: *Freedom is found in God's presence.*

Judah's exile into Babylon brought a physical bondage to match the spiritual slavery the people were experiencing in their rebellion against God. This nation had once followed the Lord, but they had been taken captive by the world around them. They adopted practices that imprisoned their souls, separating them from God. Yahweh exiled them to Babylon to help them see their need to return to Him.

Ezekiel's book can be divided into two sections:

Ezekiel 1–32—Yahweh is withdrawing
Ezekiel 33–48—Yahweh is drawing near

In the first half of the book, we find heavy indictments. Ezekiel 6 is a good example of this.

Read Ezekiel 6:1-7 and list below some of God's judgments:

Passages about scattering bones and whoring after idols aren't often displayed on Christian T-shirts or included in social media quotes! We don't have to gloss over or bury these truths about God. We know that He is multifaceted. One name or description cannot encapsulate the wholeness of His character. While He is gracious and slow to anger, He also hates counterfeits and executes judgment. Scripture says that His anger is aroused when cheap imitations lure His people away, causing them to trade the truth about Him for a lie (Romans 1:25). Yet we find that these terrible judgments Ezekiel describes had a purpose.

What does Ezekiel 6:7 reveal God's purpose to be in all this destruction?

The phrase "You shall know that I am the Lord" is repeated at least fifty times in the Book of Ezekiel as well as sprinkled throughout the Old Testament. The Almighty Creator of the universe, who is all-knowing, all-powerful, and all-present, desired that the nation of Israel would know and honor Him. He doesn't stand at a distance watching His chosen people follow counterfeits without getting involved. He got angry because He cares.

Let's also remember that this destruction didn't come out of nowhere. In Leviticus 26, we read that the Lord had clearly laid out blessings for obedience and punishment for disobedience. If the people failed to follow His decrees, He said, "And I myself will devastate the land, so that your enemies who settle in it shall be appalled at it" (Leviticus 26:32 ESV). Ezekiel 6 records an account of the Lord doing what He said He would do.

Yahweh loved His people too much to let them live with counterfeits. They were prisoners of their sin long before they became prisoners in Babylon.

Let's bring this a little closer to home. What are some ways that we today are held captive because of sin?

We can be amazing people who love God and also struggle with addictions to food, alcohol, drugs, pornography, gossip, people pleasing, video games, or any number of vices that can enslave us if we aren't careful. We must evaluate often because counterfeits are good at deceiving us. We don't usually realize where we are settling for fakes because they are designed to mimic the real thing.

Take a moment to ask yourself this question: Where might I be held captive in sin that is keeping me from knowing God better?

During some difficult seasons where I had fallen into patterns of gossip, people pleasing, and exclusivity in friendships, my sins were exposed. It was very painful, but there is great power when sin is brought into the light. If you feel a nudge from the Holy Spirit regarding any areas of bondage in your life right now, would you reach out to someone for help? Call a friend, Bible study leader, pastor, or counselor and share your struggle. Remember that freedom is found in God's presence, and He longs for us to draw near to Him.

God's messages through Ezekiel were bitter to swallow, but they didn't end without hope. In Ezekiel 33, we see a turning point after a messenger brings the report to Babylon that Jerusalem has fallen (Ezekiel 33:21). After the physical battle was over, the Lord spoke tenderly to His broken people.

Read Ezekiel 39:25-29 and mark the statements below True (T) or False (F). (If you want, you can correct the false statements by crossing out words and inserting others to make them true.)

_____ 1. God will end the captivity of the people.

_____ 2. God will have vengeance on all Israel.

_____ 3. The people will make excuses for their past shame and unfaithfulness.

_____ 4. The people will come home to live in peace in their own land with no one to bother them.

_____ 5. God will display His holiness among Israel for all the nations to see.

_____ 6. God will leave some of His people behind.

_____ 7. God will never again turn His face from His people.

_____ 8. God will pour out His Spirit upon the people of Babylon.

Answers: 1. T 2. F 3. F 4. T 5. T 6. F 7. T 8. F

This time the phrase "Then you will know that I am the Lord" was associated with blessings rather than judgment. What blessings from God can you celebrate right now?

These promises didn't come to fruition overnight for the people of Judah. The prophet Jeremiah had said that their captivity would last for seventy years, and it did. They lived with hope that they would one day return to their beloved city of Jerusalem. Yahweh continued to promise a future hope through Ezekiel, and the last chapter reveals a description of the future for this city.

Read Ezekiel 48:35 in the margin and underline the name of the city.

The name for the city of Jerusalem is God's name Yahweh Shammah, "The LORD is there." What we find here is that God will forever reside with His people. He is not absent; He is present. If we are in rebellion, He is wooing us back. For the nation of Judah, He used exile as a way to help them see their spiritual poverty. When they were broken and humbled in the process, He gave them hope for restoration.

Whether we are captives spiritually because of our own bad decisions or are experiencing what feels like bondage in our circumstances, God will use every season to help us know Him. He is Yahweh Shammah, The Lord Is There. The ultimate display of His desire to be near His people came through the sacrifice of His own Son (John 3:16). We now live under the new covenant of grace through the blood of Christ. Let's end our time today with some Scriptures that remind us of His constant presence in our lives.

Read the following Scriptures, and note in the space below how they encourage you today.

The high and lofty one who lives in eternity,
*   the Holy One, says this:*
"I live in the high and holy place
*   with those whose spirits are contrite and humble.*
I restore the crushed spirit of the humble
*   and revive the courage of those with repentant hearts.*
                                                    (Isaiah 57:15)

"The distance around the entire city will be 6 miles. And from that day the name of the city will be 'The LORD Is There.'"
(Ezekiel 48:35)

Extra Insight

Scholars have made connections between the Jerusalem described in the final chapters of Ezekiel and the heavenly city in Revelation. While they have some similar characteristics, they are not identical.

If you look for me wholeheartedly, you will find me.

(Jeremiah 29:13)

²⁷*"His purpose was for the nations to seek after God and perhaps feel their way toward him and find him—though he is not far from any one of us.* ²⁸*For in him we live and move and exist. As some of your own poets have said, 'We are his offspring.'"*

(Acts 17:27-28)

"I will never fail you.
  I will never abandon you."

(Hebrews 13:5b)

I heard a loud shout from the throne, saying, "Look, God's home is now among his people! He will live with them, and they will be his people. God himself will be with them."

(Revelation 21:3)

Captivity can come in many forms, but freedom is found in God's presence. Let us not conform to the captivity of this world but focus on the future knowing God will never leave or abandon us!

Behold

Yahweh Shammah is the Lord who is there for us.

Believe

Write a statement of belief:

Because you are always with me, I _____.

Bloom

When we know that freedom is found in God's presence, we want to draw near. Brother Lawrence wrote a short book that has become a Christian classic called *The Practice of the Presence of God*. Lawrence says this: "Let us occupy ourselves entirely in knowing God. The more we know Him, the more we will desire to know Him. As love increases with knowledge, the more we know God, the more we will truly love Him. We will learn to love Him equally in times of distress or in times of great joy."[20] Sometimes life is full of trials and other times packed with blessings. When we embrace Yahweh Shammah, The Lord Is There, we slow down and remind ourselves of God's presence. Throughout the day, let's practice His presence as we work, drive, talk with others, and do whatever we have to do, remembering The Lord Is There.

Talk with God

Yahweh Shammah, thank You for being present in my life. Expose any counterfeits that are keeping me captive. I want to turn from my sin and turn toward You, yielding to Your Spirit. I believe that my future is secure in Your hands. Help me today to practice Your presence and grow to know and love You more. Amen.

Memory Verse Exercise

Read the Memory Verse on page 108 several times, and then fill in the blanks below as you recite it:

_____ _____, O _____, _____ _____;
_____ _____, O _____, is _____ to _____
_____.

(Psalm 135:13)

Big Idea

Freedom is found in God's presence, Yahweh Shammah.

Weekly Wrap Up

Review the Big Idea for each day, and then write any personal application that comes to mind.

Day 1: Yahweh Shalom—The Lord Is Peace
Big Idea: We don't create peace; we receive it from Yahweh Shalom.

Personal Application:_____

_____

Day 2: Yahweh Sabaoth—The Lord of Heaven's Armies
Big Idea: We can find strength in life's battles as we trust Yahweh Sabaoth, the Lord of Heaven's Armies.

Personal Application:_____

_____

Day 3: Yahweh Raah—The Lord My Shepherd
Big Idea: Yahweh Raah wants to lovingly shepherd His people and offers contentment, restoration, guidance, and protection.

Personal Application:_____

_____

Day 4: Yahweh Tsidkenu – The Lord Is Our Righteousness
Big Idea: Yahweh Tsidkenu is righteousness, and He makes us righteous through Christ.

Personal Application:_____

_____

Day 5: Yahweh Shammah—The Lord Is There
Big Idea: Freedom is found in God's presence, Yahweh Shammah.

Personal Application:_____

_____

Video Viewer Guide: Week 4

Judges 6:11-16

We don't create ______________. We ______________ it from God.

God's presence plus His promises lead us to ______________.

Philippians 4:6-7

Philippians 4:8

Peace comes when we choose to ______________ instead of ______________.

Judges 6:23-24

Week 5

ADONAI, ABBA, HOLY SPIRIT

Adonai, Abba, Ruwach, Holy Spirit–Teacher, Holy Spirit–Comforter

Memory Verse

"For God is Spirit, so those who worship him must worship in spirit and in truth."
(John 4:24)

Day 1: Adonai—Master

Scripture Focus

Genesis 15:1-8;
Exodus 4:10-13;
Joshua 7:6-8; Judges
6:13-17

So far in our study we have explored the El and Yahweh names of God, and we've discovered that understanding God's names expands our view of God, helping us to know Him better. Throughout our study, our goal has not been merely to acquire information, but to answer the invitation to a deeper relationship with our Creator. This week we will study two names for God—Adonai and Abba—that do not fall into the El or Yahweh groupings, and then we will spend the rest of the week on names associated with the Spirit of God, which will lead us to our final week on the names of Jesus. I hope you've got your seat belt buckled for these last two weeks of power-packed names!

As we prepare to dive into our name for today, I want to set the stage with the metaphor of driving to illustrate what happens when a person chooses to become a Christ-follower. We hand over the keys to our lives and allow God to be in the driver's seat. His precepts will now govern how we spend our time, money, and words. To become a passenger means that we allow God to be the *master* in our lives.

In what ways do you see followers of Christ allowing God to have control in their lives?

When we yield to God's ways over our own ways, we allow God to be the master in our lives. This represents a struggle for us, because after deciding to become a Christian, we often fall back into old habits of wanting control. While we say Jesus is our Master, oftentimes what we want is for Him to be a fixer. I want to keep driving my life, but when I get in a jam, I hope Jesus will help me out. Other times, I find myself a back seat driver, telling God how my life should be run. Sometimes I flat out refuse to let God in the car, disobeying what I know to be right. None of us perfectly obeys God as master in our lives.

Today we will discover this truth: *yielding to God's sovereign rule over us brings freedom rather than bondage.*

Adonai is a name found throughout the Old Testament and is one that highlights God's Sovereign authority. Adonai is the plural of the Hebrew word *adon*, which means "lord" or "master."[1] Rulership and ownership are associated with this word. We find *adon* used in Scripture to refer to human relationships between servant and master when used in its singular form. Like Elohim, the plurality of the word elevates it as a name for our God. Adonai reveals His character as a master having authority over His creation. When we approach this name from a modern mind-set, we might feel a bit unsettled.

What comes to mind when you think of a master or someone who has lordship and authority over another?

The English words *master* and *lord* can drum up visions of slave drivers in the Deep South before the Civil War, or an authoritarian view of marriage where husbands rule and mistreat their wives. Even if your ideas are less extreme than those, it's important for us to understand that Adonai's position of Lord and Master highlights His intention to provide, protect, guard, lead, and care for His servants. To understand better, we need some insight into a human master's relationships during the days of the original audience who first heard God reveal Himself as Adonai.

Strange as it may seem to us, during biblical times the purchased slave had greater status and security than that of a hired servant.[2] The slave was included in holy day celebrations and provided for by his master. In a culture that values autonomy and free will, we might struggle to wrap our minds around this concept of freedom through submission.

Putting ourselves willfully under the authority of a master seems counterintuitive. We lose control and must surrender our wills to someone else. However, when that "someone else" is Adonai, we can find ultimate freedom. He protects, provides, and sometimes corrects like a good master.

The first mention of Adonai occurs in Genesis 15 in the middle of the story of Abraham that we've encountered in our previous weeks of study. God had promised Abraham a son when he was seventy-five years old (Genesis 12). When a decade had passed with no pregnancy, Abraham had questions for God regarding the many descendants that He promised to a childless couple.

Read Genesis 15:1-8 and write below how Abraham addresses God in verses 2 and 8:

Extra Insight

A ten-year gap separates Genesis 12 and 15.

Your translation may say "Sovereign LORD" (NLT, NIV), or "LORD God" (KJV), "O Lord GOD" (ESV, NASB). The original Hebrew words are *Adonai Yahweh*. Abraham addressed God as Yahweh, the Self-Existent One, but added the word *Adonai* appealing to Him as Master. He wasn't cowering in fear under God's authority. He was humbly appealing to his Master with questions. This supports the Hebrew understanding of a master as an approachable authority. In fact, many great people of God used the name Adonai when making an appeal to God as master.

As you read the following passages, identify the person who called on Adonai and their plea to their master:

¹⁰But Moses pleaded with the Lᴏʀᴅ [Yahweh], "O Lord [Adonai], I'm not very good with words. I never have been, and I'm not now, even though you have spoken to me. I get tongue-tied, and my words get tangled."

¹¹Then the Lᴏʀᴅ [Yahweh] asked Moses, "Who makes a person's mouth? Who decides whether people speak or do not speak, hear or do not hear, see or do not see? Is it not I, the Lᴏʀᴅ? ¹²Now go! I will be with you as you speak, and I will instruct you in what to say."

¹³But Moses again pleaded, "Lord [Adonai], please! Send anyone else."

(Exodus 4:10-13)

Person:

Plea:

⁶Joshua and the elders of Israel tore their clothing in dismay, threw dust on their heads, and bowed face down to the ground before the Ark of the Lᴏʀᴅ [Yahweh] until evening. ⁷Then Joshua cried out, "Oh, Sovereign Lᴏʀᴅ [Yahweh], why did you bring us across the Jordan River if you are going to let the Amorites kill us? If only we had been content to stay on the other side! ⁸Lord [Adonai], what can I say now that Israel has fled from its enemies?

(Joshua 7:6-8)

Person:

Plea:

¹³"Sir," Gideon replied, "if the Lᴏʀᴅ [Yahweh] is with us, why has all this happened to us? And where are all the miracles our ancestors told us about? Didn't they say, 'The Lᴏʀᴅ [Yahweh] brought us up out of Egypt'? But now the Lᴏʀᴅ [Yahweh] has abandoned us and handed us over to the Midianites."

¹⁴Then the Lᴏʀᴅ [Yahweh] turned to him and said, "Go with the strength you have, and rescue Israel from the Midianites. I am sending you!"

¹⁵"But Lord [Adonai]," Gideon replied, "how can I rescue Israel? My clan is the weakest in the whole tribe of Manasseh, and I am the least in my entire family!"

¹⁶The Lᴏʀᴅ [Yahweh] said to him, "I will be with you. And you will destroy the Midianites as if you were fighting against one man."

(Judges 6:13-16)

Ancient scribes who copied the Old Testament did not say the word *Yahweh* aloud when they encountered it in the text. They substituted *Adonai* in its place to preserve the holiness of the name Yahweh.[3] Adonai is found more than four hundred times in the Bible.[4]

Person

Plea:

What do the situations of Moses, Joshua, and Gideon have in common?

Whether these texts are familiar stories or new to you, how does seeing the different names of God in the text enhance your reading?

Each person was in a confusing situation. They wanted to yield to God's instructions, but they would have handled the circumstances differently if they were in the driver's seat. They yielded to God as master, calling His name Adonai and admitting that they needed guidance.

Can you think of a time in your life when following God's instructions left you with questions? If so, write about it briefly below:

Extra Insight

Jesus used the illustration of a master often, such as, "Students are not greater than their teacher, and slaves are not greater than their master. Students are to be like their teacher, and slaves are to be like their master" (Matthew 10:24-25a).

Moses thought his Master should choose a better speaker. Joshua wondered why his Lord allowed them to lose a battle. Gideon didn't understand the suffering of his people and didn't feel qualified to lead them. Each one cried out to Adonai. They didn't see Him as an authoritarian despot who couldn't be approached. Instead, they dialogued and used His name "Adonai" almost as if reminding Him that He was supposed to be a Master and take care of them.

If we had time to keep reading each of their stories, we would discover that Moses, Joshua, and Gideon ultimately yielded to Adonai in obedience even without all of their questions answered. We can learn from them to submit to God's instructions even when we don't fully comprehend them.

Can you identify an area where you need to submit to God as Master in your life? If so, write about it briefly below:

I need to submit to His Lordship when it comes to my time, thoughts, and attitudes. The wonderful thing is that God doesn't ask us to do it on our own. I hope you noticed in our reading today how the Lord came alongside those He called to serve Him. He wants to do the same for you and me. We can willingly hand Him the keys to the driver's seat of our lives knowing that His way is best.

Behold

God revealed Himself as Adonai, our Lord and Master.

Believe

Write a statement of belief:

I believe that you are Adonai, and I desire today to yield to Your way as I _____.

Bloom

What differentiates us as Christians is that we acknowledge the lordship of a higher power. We don't claim to do what is right in our own eyes; we look to God as revealed in the Scriptures as the One who sets the standards. The more we trust Him, the more we will yield to His Sovereignty in our lives. Ask Adonai to be master over your day as you seek to serve His agenda over your own.

Talk with God

Adonai, You have all authority in heaven and earth, and yet you are a loving Master who cares for your servants. I am your servant, and I yield to your ways over mine. I want to navigate my own path, but it never turns out well when I do. Help me to trust that freedom is found in obeying You. Amen.

Memory Verse Exercise

Read the Memory Verse on page 140 several times, and then fill in the blanks below as you recite it:

"For God is _____, so those who worship him must worship in spirit and in truth."

(John 4:24)

Day 2: Abba—Father

Throughout our study we are discovering that God progressively reveals His character in the Bible through His names. The New Testament sheds even greater light on the plurality of God, showing us that He is the triune Father,

Big Idea

Adonai is a loving Master to be obeyed, even when we have questions.

Scripture Focus

Mark 14:36;
Romans 8:15-17;
Galatians 4:4-7

Son, and Holy Spirit. Although we don't find the word *trinity* in the Bible, many passages give a clear picture of God's threefold personage. Matthew 28:19, for example, says, "Therefore, go and make disciples of all the nations, baptizing them in the name of the Father and the Son and the Holy Spirit." Notice that the word *name* in this verse is singular. In a way that words cannot fully capture, we serve one God expressed in three persons.

For the remainder of our study we will camp on the three persons of the Trinity, and today we will focus on the Father.

My husband became a father twenty-three years ago, and since then my children have called him "Dad" or "Daddy." In fact, they've called him that so much that I often refer to him with that name. When we are discussing something pertaining to the kids, I might say, "Daddy, what do you think?" Or other times my children will ask me something and I'll tell them I'll have to check with Dad.

For better or worse, the way my husband fathers our children will have an impact on the lens they use as they consider God as Father. Our relationship with our human fathers can have an impact on how we see our heavenly One.

In one word, how would you describe your relationship with your dad?

Maybe you said "nonexistent," "close," "difficult," or even "complicated." As we look today at God's name Abba, which means father, we need to remember that while our earthly fathers are imperfect, He is a perfect father. Even the best of fathers disappoints his children from time to time. Earthly paternal relationships can color our perspective when it comes to our view of God. Studying God's Father qualities helps us to have a more accurate view of His heart toward us despite any human father wounds we may have sustained. Knowing God as Abba Father can also heal the damage we've experienced from our earthly fathers.

We find many fatherly references in the Old Testament concerning human relationships, but God is referenced as Father only fifteen times there. Of those references, God is depicted as a Father either in a general sense as the Father of the nation of Israel or in reference to specific individuals.

Read the following passages and then complete the exercise on the next page:

Is this the way you repay the LORD, you foolish and senseless people? Isn't he your Father who created you? Has he not made you and established you?

(Deuteronomy 32:6)

Father to the fatherless, defender of widows—
this is God, whose dwelling is holy.

(Psalm 68:5)

Extra Insights

Abba is an Aramaic word used in the Hebrew language as an intimate way to address a father.[5]

Perhaps the metaphor of God as father was scarce in the Old Testament "due to its frequent use in the ancient Near East where it was used in various fertility religions and carried heavy sexual overtones."[6]

Surely you are still our Father!
  Even if Abraham and Jacob would disown us,
LORD, you would still be our Father.
  You are our Redeemer from ages past.
                                        (Isaiah 63:16)

"I thought to myself,
  'I would love to treat you as my own children!'
I wanted nothing more than to give you this beautiful land—
  the finest possession in the world.
I looked forward to your calling me 'Father,'
  and I wanted you never to turn from me."
                                        (Jeremiah 3:19)

Put a check mark next to qualities of God displayed in these verses:

_____1. Creator

_____2. Quick-tempered

_____3. Holy (set apart)

_____4. Tired

_____5. Protects and provides (fathers) orphans

_____6. Faithful Redeemer

_____7. Work-a-holic

_____8. Desires His people to turn to Him

God is not only our holy Creator but also a protector and provider—a Father to orphans—who faithfully redeems and desires His people to return to Him. God as Father may not be a prevalent concept in the Old Testament, but we cannot deny its presence. The New Testament brings the Old Testament hints of God's fatherhood to center stage. Jesus refers to God as Father more than 150 times in the Gospel of John alone. Most often, Jesus uses the Greek word *pater* for His Heavenly Father.

We find the specific name Abba used only three times. This is the Aramaic word for "father" and serves as an informal term focused on the relational aspect of the father/child connection. Some have suggested it would be the equivalent of "papa" or "daddy,"[7] which would mean that Jesus revealed the Father not as a ruling patriarch of His people but as a tender and gracious daddy. In any case, He demonstrated an intimate family relationship with the One that many of His peers revered from a distance.

Some controversy regarding the word *Abba* and its origins exists within scholarly circles. "The thought of Abba being an Aramaic way of saying 'Daddy' was the suggestion of a 20th century scholar, Jeremias, and was intended to be only this— a suggestion.... Regardless of the etymological evidence, modern Hebrew today uses the word Abba as an intimate reference to father (daddy or papa), so it is also possible that oral tradition has carried this down from native Hebrew speakers throughout the generations."[8]

Read Mark 14:32-36 and describe the situation when Jesus cried out to God as "Abba, Father" in your own words:

I love the thought that when His soul was crushed with grief to the point of death, Jesus cried out for His daddy. He expressed emotion over the suffering that He knew lay ahead of Him. Ultimately, He asked for the will of the Father over the pain of the moment. Like Jesus, we can cry out to God as Abba when the weight of trouble feels heavy on our souls.

Take a moment to consider what is weighing on you right now. Then write a brief prayer about it to your Abba Father below:

While Adonai is our master, He is also our Abba. He sees our pain and invites us to come to Him. Abba did not take away the cup of suffering from Jesus, and He doesn't always fix our situations either. He works for the ultimate good in our lives just as He did for His own Son. Christ submitted Himself to Abba even when it meant drinking a cup of suffering, and we can learn from His example to put our trust in our heavenly Father, knowing that He always has our ultimate good in mind.

The apostle Paul also used Abba in two of his letters to churches to teach them about their identity as children of God.

Read Romans 8:15-17 and answer the following questions:

What kind of spirit have you *not* received? (v. 15)

What has God done so that you can now call Him Abba Father? (v. 15)

As children, what benefit do we receive from Abba? (v. 17)

What will we share with Jesus in addition to His glory? (v. 17)

It cost God something to adopt us as His children. He sent Jesus knowing the pain He would endure. After Jesus pleaded with God the Father, the plan didn't change. Abba allowed His only Son to suffer in order to adopt us as children. As children, we can call on God as Father when we face suffering knowing that He hears us. His presence gives us comfort.

How does the truth about your identity as a child of God encourage you today?

We will share in Christ's glory, but this passage warns us that we also will share in His suffering. We live in a culture that wants an easy button for everything. We consider questions such as these:

- How can I lose weight without giving up the pleasure of food?
- How can I get out of debt and still buy what I want?
- How can I make money and not work too hard?
- How can I gain godly character but never endure suffering?

The path of least resistance doesn't bring the results we desire. Jesus calls us to mimic His example in the sacrificial life. He said, "If any of you wants to be my follower, you must give up your own way, take up your cross daily, and follow me" (Luke 9:23). Taking up a cross means choosing the hard road of suffering at times. Like Jesus, we can ask Abba for another way, but ultimately, we must defer to His judgment.

After telling the Roman church that they would share in Christ's suffering as God's children, Paul reminded them of this, "Yet what we suffer now is nothing compared to the glory he will reveal to us later" (Romans 8:18). If you are a follower of Jesus, your suffering has an expiration date. Whether your season is one of glory or suffering right now, you can cry out to God as your Abba Father.

The final mention of Abba in the Bible is found in Paul's Letter to the Galatians.

Read Galatians 4:4-7. What metaphor does Paul use to emphasize our freedom?

Complete verse 7 by filling in the blanks with your own name:

Now _____ is no longer a slave but God's own child. And since _____ is his child, God has made _____ his heir.

The name Abba highlights our position as God's child. Paul used the metaphor of slavery to emphasize our freedom. He didn't use only the Greek word *pater* for father like most of the New Testament writers, but he chose *Abba Pater*. God is our papa, our daddy. When we embrace our identity as a beloved child who is loved and treasured, it changes us. We act, speak, and live from our identity. Today, I pray that you know and feel loved and treasured by your Abba!

Behold

Abba Father has adopted us as His children through Christ.

Believe

Write a statement of belief:

Because I have been adopted by Abba, I am _____ _____.

Bloom

What perspective do you gain today as you see yourself as the adopted child of God?

Whether our earthly fathers were great examples or left us with challenges to overcome in our view of God, we have a perfect Abba Father who loves us. He has adopted us as children and has given us a rich inheritance through Christ.

Talk with God

Abba Father, I cry out to You. I don't always understand the struggles I encounter. I am so grateful to share in the glory of your Son but also understand that it means I will share in His suffering as well. Help me yield to Your will even when it's really difficult. You are my daddy, and I am so grateful that You have adopted me as your child. Amen.

Memory Verse Exercise

Read the Memory Verse on page 140 several times, and then fill in the blanks below as you recite it:

For God is _____, so those who _____ him must worship in spirit and in truth.

(John 4:24)

Day 3: Ruwach—The Spirit of God

Big Idea

Jesus revealed the Father not as a ruling patriarch of His people but as Abba, a tender and gracious daddy.

Scripture Focus

1 Samuel 10:1-8; 16:13-14; Acts 2:1-13

Today I asked the Holy Spirit to give me creative ideas and guide my thoughts as I studied so that I could write about Him. I can't say that I've ever heard His audible voice, but I sense His leading when I pray for others or wrestle with Scripture. When I review articles I've written in the past or listen to a teaching session I've previously recorded, I often whisper thanks to the Holy Spirit, knowing He supplied all the energy and ideas. At times the Holy Spirit has been associated with miraculous demonstrations or intense emotions, but I have found my personal experience with Him to be better described by gentle nudging. In my life His power has been revealed in quiet, unassuming ways.

The Holy Spirit of God might be the most controversial topic we will cover in our study of God's names. Christians across the globe disagree on the way His gifts should be used and how He works in people's lives. I pray that as we look to the Scriptures we will not focus on our differing views. Instead, I want to ask you to invite the Spirit of God to reveal Himself more fully through our study over the next three days.

Write a short prayer to God's Spirit below, inviting Him to reveal Himself to you through your study:

In Genesis 1:2, we encounter the Hebrew word *ruwach* to describe the Spirit of God. "The earth was formless and empty, and darkness covered the deep waters. And the Spirit of God was hovering over the surface of the waters" (Genesis 1:2). *Ruwach* means "wind, breath, mind, spirit" and, of course, would not have been identified by the original audience as a member of the Trinity.[9] However, with progressive revelation, we can look back and see the Holy Spirit at work from the very beginning.

God's Spirit was involved in Creation and very much at work during Old Testament times. However, He did not indwell every follower of God; instead, He empowered certain people for specific tasks. Today we will be turning to many different passages to discover what the Old Testament reveals to us about the Holy Spirit.

Read Exodus 31:1-5. How did the Spirit help Bezalel in this passage?

Extra Insight

Ruwach, when referenced as "Spirit or spirit," is mentioned in the Old Testament 232 times.[10]

The Spirit of God filled Bezalel, enabling him and many other craftsmen for the work of building the tabernacle according to God's instructions. The period of the Judges also gives additional insight into the work of God's Spirit before He began to indwell believers in Christ.

Look up the following passages and note each judge and what he accomplished through the Spirit of the Lord:

Judges 3:9-11

Judges 6:33-35

Judges 15:14

Othniel, Gideon, and Samson were filled with God's Spirit so they could fight physical battles. The Holy Spirit came for a specific purpose to help an individual with a specific task.

From the verses we've read so far in Exodus and Judges, how would you summarize what the Spirit of God enabled people to do?

From creating beauty from raw materials to helping leaders command armies against an enemy, the Spirit equipped people to carry out their God-given callings.

Can you identify a way in which the Holy Spirit has empowered *you* to use your gifts? If so, describe it below:

Even though the Holy Spirit's role in the Old and New Testament isn't identical, His work remains consistent in enabling God's people with God's power. Let's jump from the time of the judges to the biblical narrative when kings ruled the nation of Israel to identify some characteristics of the Spirit's work in the lives of Saul and David.

Read 1 Samuel 10:1-8 and 1 Samuel 16:13-14. What do you learn about the Holy Spirit from Saul's experiences?

While the Spirit of the Lord came upon Saul, it also departed from him. The Lord then chose a shepherd boy named David to be the next king of Israel. He understood that God's Spirit was a powerful gift but not a guarantee. After a sin of adultery was exposed in David's life, he prayed these words, "Do not banish me from your presence, and don't take your Holy Spirit from me" (Psalm 51:11). David's prayer was answered, and he continued to serve God despite his many failings. The Holy Spirit was taken from Saul because of habitual unrepentant sin but remained with David as he humbled himself before the Lord. God determined whether to give or remove His Spirit in the lives of specific individuals.

What we've read so far may cause us to deduce that the Spirit was reserved for special people like kings, prophets, or judges. However, the future role of the Spirit of God was foretold by the prophet Joel.

Read Joel 2:28-29 in the margin and describe what God promised to do in the future regarding His Spirit:

28"Then, after doing all those things,
I will pour out my Spirit upon all people.
Your sons and daughters will prophesy.
Your old men will dream dreams, and your young men will see visions.
29In those days I will pour out my Spirit even on servants—men and women alike."
(Joel 2:28-29)

Joel said that in the future the Spirit of God would be poured out on God's servants, including both men and women. The Holy Spirit wouldn't be reserved for a few special individuals, but for all who would believe the gospel of Christ. Jesus said that when He left, God would send the Holy Spirit.

Read Acts 2:1-13 and answer the following questions:

What holy day were the believers celebrating? (v. 1)

What did they hear? (v. 2)

What did they see? (v. 3)

What ability did the Holy Spirit provide? (v. 4)

What did those in the crowd assume about the people filled with the Spirit? (v. 13)

Some assumed that an excess of alcohol explained what was happening here. Yet these people were not overcome by drinks but by the Spirit of God. In the next few verses, Peter quoted the prophet Joel and explained that his words were fulfilled on that day. The events of Acts 2 also satisfied the promise of Jesus. While Jesus was teaching His disciples, He had told them, "And I will ask the Father, and he will give you another Advocate, who will never leave you. He is the Holy Spirit, who leads into all truth" (John 14:16-17a).

Jesus said the Holy Spirit would come and never leave; He is our Advocate who will lead us into all truth! In fact, Jesus said it was better that He return to heaven so the Spirit would come (John 16:7).

What similarities do you notice between the work of the Holy Spirit in the Old and New Testaments?

What difference(s) do you notice between the work of the Holy Spirit in the Old and New Testaments?

God's Spirit empowered and strengthened people whether they lived before or after the coming of the Messiah. While only certain individuals in the Old

Testament were given the Holy Spirit for specific tasks or purposes and for varying durations, after Christ ascended to heaven and the Spirit came powerfully at Pentecost (Acts 2), things changed, with the Holy Spirit continually indwelling every person who follows Jesus.

Paul wrote letters to churches and individuals reminding them that the Holy Spirit dwelled within them (1 Corinthians 3:16; 2 Timothy 1:14). He used the Greek word *oikeo* to describe the Holy Spirit living in the New Testament believer. As one source notes, "The significance of the term *oikeo* is that it speaks of *permanency*. The idea is that the Holy Spirit takes up residency in believers [those who follow Jesus]—forever. He doesn't just pass through. He makes us His home. He comes to stay."[11]

We will unpack some of the key tenets of the Holy Spirit found in the New Testament in the next two days. For now, let's focus on the fact that He will never leave those of us who follow Jesus because He dwells within us.

How does the continual indwelling of the Holy Spirit encourage you in your walk with God?

For Jesus to say that it was better for Him to leave so that the Spirit could come blows my mind. It seems to me that having Jesus in a human body here on earth where He could teach and show us by example would be more beneficial. Yet He said the Spirit would be better. When I read about how God's Holy Spirit equipped people in the Old Testament to build and create as well as fight their battles, I am reminded of His power to help us do what God asks us to do. Knowing that He continually lives in me gives me courage to be strong because I am not alone. I don't have to figure out everything by myself. The Spirit of the Living God lives in me, and if you are a Christ-follower, He lives in You.

Behold

The Spirit of the Living God dwells within and promises never to leave us who follow Jesus.

Believe

Because of the permanence and power of the Holy Spirit living in me, I believe _____.

Bloom

Take a moment to consider how the reality of God's Spirit living in you changes your perspective on the week ahead. In what areas of your life do you feel God's quiet nudge to act, change, or even slow down?

God has not left us here to figure out how to follow Him using only our logic and emotions. He has given us His Holy Spirit so that we might be empowered to live out His commands. This Spirit came upon us when we first decided to follow Jesus, and He has taken up residency within us. Let these truths wash over you in a fresh way as you honor God today!

Talk with God

Holy Spirit, thank You for living in me. Help me to yield to You. Show me what it means to let You control my life. Empower me to do the things You want me to do. I can't navigate my life, but I know You can. Amen.

Memory Verse Exercise

Read the Memory Verse on page 140 several times, and then fill in the blanks below as you recite it:

For God is _____, so those who _____ him must worship in _____ and in _____.

(John 4:24)

Scripture Focus

Romans 8:26-27; 1 Corinthians 2:10-16

Big Idea

Although the Holy Spirit's roles in the Old and New Testaments aren't identical, His work remains consistent in empowering God's people.

Day 4: Holy Spirit—Teacher

My mother and both of my sisters have backgrounds in education. All of them have been schoolteachers at different times in their lives. They are able to take difficult concepts and break them down in a way that students can understand. My brother, who writes a popular blog with a large computer company, credits the success of his blog to the same skills that my mother and sisters possess. He has the ability to write a step-by-step process for the average person to understand when it comes to dealing with complex computer issues.

The Holy Spirit has many roles in our lives, but today we will focus on His ability to teach us. Just as my brother's blog breaks down information to make it usable, so the Holy Spirit helps us apply Scripture in real life. He is not an impersonal force, so we should never refer to the Spirit as "it." He is an entity that can be resisted (Acts 7:51), quenched (1 Thessalonians 5:19), and grieved (Ephesians 4:30).

Before we go further in our study of God's Spirit, take a moment to reflect on what you've learned about Him in the past. Where did you first hear about the Holy Spirit, and what initial impressions did you have of Him?

Maybe your parents or friends explained the Holy Spirit to you. Perhaps you heard teaching about Him at your church. Or you may have discovered Him through reading the Bible. As a Teacher, He wants to help us understand God's commands so that He can produce good things in our lives. Scripture says that when we yield to Him, we will bloom with good fruit.

22But the Holy Spirit produces this kind of fruit in our lives: love, joy, peace, patience, kindness, goodness, faithfulness, 23gentleness, and self-control. There is no law against these things!
(Galatians 5:22-23)

Read Galatians 5:22-23 in the margin and list one of the qualities of the fruit of the Spirit that stands out to you today:

_____

I know I need more of the Holy Spirit's leading in my life because I want more of this fruit to exude from my thoughts, words, and actions. So how do we get it? I wish I could write the five-step secret to allowing the Holy Spirit to take over, but unfortunately there is no checklist. Remember that He is a person living within us, so we are talking about a relationship that might look different for each of us. However, since we know that the Spirit is a teacher, we can focus on what it looks like to be a better student.

What are some qualities that help a student learn best from a teacher?

I thought of traits such as being humble, listening intently, and valuing the teacher's knowledge. Perhaps you thought of others. The most important posture for a student is teachability. If we think we already know everything and aren't willing to make life changes, we won't glean much from the teacher's instruction. As we focus on three ways that the Holy Spirit teaches us, let's evaluate our teachability in each area so that we can grow as students:

- He guides us in prayer.
- He reveals the truth of God.
- He directs us in decisions.

He Guides Us in Prayer

First of all, prayer is an area in which the Holy Spirit can help us.

Read Romans 8:26-27 below and underline some phrases that tell how the Holy Spirit helps us in prayer:

²⁶And the Holy Spirit helps us in our weakness. For example, we don't know what God wants us to pray for. But the Holy Spirit prays for us with groanings that cannot be expressed in words. ²⁷And the Father who knows all hearts knows what the Spirit is saying, for the Spirit pleads for us believers in harmony with God's own will.

(Romans 8:26-27)

When I've been at a loss to know what to pray, I have experienced these internal groans and sensed the Holy Spirit interceding for me. Can you think of a situation when you knew you needed prayer but couldn't find the words? If anything comes to mind, record it below:

I've noticed that many prayers recorded in Scripture contain requests for direction, salvation, or growth rather than quick fixes to temporary problems. My prayer journal is often the opposite. I mostly ask Jesus to "fix it" for me and those I love. I am trying to grow in this area, so I am admitting my weakness. That seems to be the first step according to these verses in Romans. We won't look to the Holy Spirit to help us in prayer if we don't realize our need for His assistance. Just as a drowning victim has to stop flailing and give up before she can be rescued, we have to recognize our weakness and come to Him. Then the Spirit can pray in harmony with God's will on our behalf.

Now let's remember that prayer is talking to God. There is no "wrong" way to do it. The content of our prayers reveals our hearts, and we can connect with God on a deeper level as we learn more about prayer from the Holy Spirit.

How might you be a more teachable student under the instruction of the Holy Spirit regarding prayer? Write some ideas below:

He Reveals the Truth of God

Another way the Holy Spirit teaches us has to do with our understanding of spiritual truth. The apostle Paul wrote to the church at Corinth that we need the Holy Spirit to open our minds to the truths of God.

Look up 1 Corinthians 2:10-16 in your Bible and fill in the blanks (answers may vary based on your translation):

The Holy Spirit shows us God's deep _____. (v. 10)

The Holy Spirit knows God's _____. (v. 11)

The Holy Spirit helps us know the wonderful things God has freely _____ us. (v. 12)

Paul and church leaders spoke _____ given by the Holy Spirit. (v. 13)

The Holy Spirit provides spiritual _____ to receive truth. (v. 14)

The Holy Spirit helps us _____ all things. (v. 15)

The Holy Spirit can help us when we don't understand something the Bible is teaching. He also provides discernment when we hear false teaching. We can dialogue with the Holy Spirit as we read the Bible or listen to a sermon so that we might understand and apply what we are learning. For the teacher/student relationship with the Holy Spirit to work, we first have to read, listen, or meditate on God's truth. Then we ask questions and receive direction as the Holy Spirit helps us process and utilize that understanding.

What would it look like for you to be a more teachable student of the Holy Spirit as the revealer of truth?

Extra Insight

See 1 John 2:27 and John 16:13 for more study on how the Holy Spirit reveals God's truth in our lives.

For me, it often looks like slowing down, evaluating, and asking more questions. I often fly through my daily reading so that I can check it off as complete. In order to be a better student, I want to spend more time in reflection, meditation, and memorization.

He Directs Us in Decisions

The Holy Spirit also directs our decisions. When I asked friends on social media to write comments about their relationship with the Holy Spirit, most wrote about His direction. They said things like this:

The Holy Spirit told me to prepare for a trip to Haiti two years ago. I had no idea when I would be going, but I prepared my heart and body. I recently got back from Haiti after spending a month there.

I truly believe it was the Holy Spirit that made me get off a plane headed to Florida when I was in pre-term labor with my daughter. Otherwise she would have been born on a plane at thirty-one weeks.

Once, my husband felt led to visit a friend who wasn't answering his phone. When he walked in the door, his friend was preparing to commit suicide. Praise God for divine intervention.

The Holy Spirit led me to check my daughter's room the day I found her journal that revealed she was depressed, cutting herself, and having suicidal thoughts. I was sitting outside when I kept getting this very insistent, intrusive "thought" out of nowhere to go check her room. I didn't even know what I was supposed to be looking for, and she had given no signs she was struggling. I'm so grateful that we were able to get her into counseling before something tragic happened!

Do you have a story about a time when you sensed the Holy Spirit directing you in some way? If so, record your experience below:

The Holy Spirit longs to direct us on right paths as we navigate our days.

Read the following verses and underline the verb associated with the Holy Spirit in each Scripture:

Then Jesus was led by the Spirit into the wilderness to be tempted there by the devil.

(Matthew 4:1)

[11][Jesus said,] "And when you are brought to trial in the synagogues and before rulers and authorities, don't worry about how to defend yourself or what to say, [12]for the Holy Spirit will teach you at that time what needs to be said."

(Luke 12:11-12)

The Holy Spirit said to Philip, "Go over and walk along beside the carriage."

(Acts 8:29)

One day as these men were worshiping the Lord and fasting, the Holy Spirit said, "Appoint Barnabas and Saul for the special work to which I have called them."

(Acts 13:2)

So I say, let the Holy Spirit guide your lives. Then you won't be doing what your sinful nature craves.

(Galatians 5:16)

What are some ways the Holy Spirit directed decisions in these verses?

The Holy Spirit told people where to go and what to say and who to put into leadership. These are just a few of many examples of how the Holy Spirit can guide our lives. When I read these passages, I wonder how the individuals knew for sure that it was the Spirit speaking to them. Most of us wrestle with whether an idea is coming from our own thoughts or is indeed a nudge from the Holy Spirit. Often, I don't realize it was the Spirit until I look back and see His direction.

What are some ways we can recognize the voice of the Holy Spirit in our lives?

Perhaps you noted confirmation through Scripture, other people, or circumstances. Or you might have written something about intentional listening or learning to recognize His voice with practice. I noticed that in Acts, the church heard the Spirit's voice as they were worshiping and fasting. Our obedience to the practices of God can help tune our ears to hear the voice of God. Other times He can be so persistent that we can't shake the gentle promptings we hear.

In what ways would you like to grow in your teachability as a student in being directed by the Holy Spirit in your daily decisions?

The Holy Spirit is a powerful name of God. I pray that drawing near to Him will awaken in us a desire to learn at the feet of this awesome Teacher.

Behold

Today we have beheld God the Holy Spirit as a teacher who guides us in prayer, reveals the truth of God, and directs us in decisions.

Believe

Write a statement of belief:

The Holy Spirit is my teacher, and I desire to learn _____

_____ .

Bloom

Look back at what you recorded in today's lesson about the ways you want to become more teachable in prayer, truth, and decisions. Attaching a new habit to an already established habit can be a helpful tool so that we put feet to our good intentions. We can look for a habit we already have in place and add a new habit we'd like to introduce, essentially stacking them together. I already read my Bible consistently, so I am adding a few minutes after I finish reading to review a weekly verse. Consider any areas where habit stacking might be helpful to you. If you drink coffee every day, maybe you spend the few moments as you are waiting for it to brew to listen quietly for the Holy Spirit. Perhaps you include in your bedtime routine a time of reflection to review your day, asking the Holy Spirit to reveal ways you can give thanks.

Write any ideas you have for habit stacking in your routine below:

The Holy Spirit of God is our teacher. He longs to instruct us as we develop into teachable students. I pray that each of us will look for ways this week to get more in tune with His voice so that we might obey His promptings.

Talk with God

Holy Spirit, I need Your help. I don't know the right way unless You show me when it comes to praying, understanding the Bible, and making daily decisions. Please guide me and allow me to hear Your voice clearly. Thank You for the gift of your presence and direction. Help me to yield to You today as I navigate conversations, appointments, and time management. Amen.

Memory Verse Exercise

Read the Memory Verse on page 140 several times, and then fill in the blanks below as you recite it:

_____ God is _____, so _____ who _____ him
must _____ in _____ and in _____.

(John 4:24)

God is _____, so _____ who _____ him must _____ in _____ and in _____.

Day 5: Holy Spirit—Comforter

Big Idea

God gave us the Holy Spirit to guide us when it comes to prayer, truth, and direction in life, so we want to be teachable students.

Yesterday I returned home from a long weekend of ministry in another state. I had been awake since 4 a.m. to catch an early flight, and I was weary physically and emotionally. Upon arriving home, I received some devastating news concerning someone I dearly love. I spent the day crying on and off. Sometimes it was hard, ugly crying, and other times I found unbidden tears escaping down my cheeks as I tried to unpack and focus on tasks in front of me.

I'm not ready to put words to the details of the situation quite yet, but trust me when I tell you that I found studying the Comforter role of the Holy Spirit today extremely relevant in my life. If you don't find yourself in a season like mine, I pray today's study will deepen your understanding so that the next time you experience grief, you can hold on to the truth that your God is a Comforter.

What are some ways we look for comfort when we feel sad or hurt?

Scripture Focus

John 15:26; 2 Corinthians 1:3-4

There can be healthy ways to seek comfort, but there also are less healthy escapes that will not bring ultimate comfort for us. The gals in the pilot study group identified these methods below that we sometimes use to seek comfort.

Draw a star beside the those things that you would label as healthy options for you when you need *real comfort*. (Keep in mind that some may be healthy for one person but unhealthy for another for some reason, while others may be healthy or unhealthy for all people.)

____ Listening to music   ____ Sleeping

____ Seeking solitude   ____ Sitting outside in creation

____ Eating food   ____ Taking a walk

_____ Reading a good book   _____ Staring into a fire or fish tank

_____ Watching movies or TV   _____ Meditating on God or Scripture

_____ Scrolling social media   _____ Being near a body of water

_____ Talking with a friend   _____ Distracting yourself with tasks

_____ Add your own idea here:

God can use some of these things at times, but ultimately He longs to be the source of our comfort. In Isaiah 40:1, we read these words, "Comfort, comfort my people, says your God." He knows that we are seeking comfort because much of life is uncomfortable. Relationships end. People die. Friends betray. Finances get tight. Children make bad choices. Scary diagnoses are given. We also encounter pesky colds, parking tickets, long work hours, and so many other wearying circumstances that cause us to seek comfort. We may find momentary relief in a bowl of ice cream or a numbing television marathon, but ultimate comfort comes from our Creator.

Read John 15:26 in your Bible and write below the word used for the Holy Spirit:

Depending on your version, you might have found:

- Advocate (NLT, NIV)
- Helper (NASB, NKJV, ESV)
- Comforter (KJV)

The Amplified Bible gives us even greater insight:

"But when the Helper (Comforter, Advocate, Intercessor—Counselor, Strengthener, Standby) comes, whom I will send to you from the Father, that is the Spirit of Truth who comes from the Father, He will testify and bear witness about Me.
(John 15:26 AMP)

The Greek word John used in this verse is _Parakletos_. Strong's Concordance reveals the definition as "summoned, called to one's side, esp. called to one's aid...one who pleads another's cause before a judge, a pleader, counsel for defense, legal assistant, an advocate...one who pleads another's cause with one, an intercessor...in the widest sense, a helper...aider, assistant."[12]

The Holy Spirit of God who indwells all believers will advocate, help, and comfort us. He comes from the Father and will reveal more of Jesus to us. This name of God encourages us that we are not alone in navigating an uncomfortable world.

Even though we have the Holy Spirit, I often feel a tension when I'm in need of comfort. I want to seek God's Spirit to comfort me, but another part of me wants an instantaneous pain block. I felt this war inside me in my distress. I longed for food, sleep, TV, or any distraction to keep from having to face painful news. When the desire for distraction passed, I wanted to conjure up a repair attempt for the situation. In these particular circumstances, there is nothing I can do or not do to "fix it." No words or actions will change what has transpired. It simply is.

I now have to choose my place of comfort. Will I allow the Holy Spirit to be my Comforter in this? Throughout the day when tears threatened, I cried out to Him. I asked for His comfort. I admitted my need. I didn't hear an audible voice or feel physical arms around me, but I did receive His comfort in these ways:

Extra Insight

The apostle John is the only one who uses *Parakletos* for the Holy Spirit in Scripture. He references the word four times in his Gospel and once in the book of 1 John.[13]

- He reminded me of truth. (This grief will pass. Nothing is so far gone that God cannot redeem it.)
- He spoke through my husband who brought me comfort. (Sean held me, mourned with me, and prayed with me.)
- I sensed His supernatural presence giving me hope. (I don't have words to describe an awareness of this Person I cannot see or touch, yet I know He is here.)

Have you ever sought comfort from God through His Holy Spirit? If so, what are some ways that you have received help in a difficult time?

Some of the responses I received on social media regarding the Holy Spirit referenced His role as Comforter. Here are a few comments that illustrate how the Spirit's comfort has been received by others:

I remember lying in bed one night with silent tears streaming so I wouldn't wake my hubby, and I prayed for comfort from the only One I could get it from. In that moment, I felt the warmest hug simply envelop me, and for the first time since my mom had died, I actually felt peace and comfort like no other feeling I had ever had.

He has spoken to me in my moments of greatest fear, pouring peace over me like a waterfall, and then held me through the aftermath so I could sing praises on the other side.

The Holy Spirit has given me a warm peace from my head to my toes when in fear of a medical procedure.

I first found the Holy Spirit as a Comforter as a broken teen coming to Christ. He then began to nurture and strengthen me. Then He insisted on realigning my heart and mind to God's Word. He is both gentle and strong.

When it comes to our relationship with the Holy Spirit, we might find different ways to receive comfort, depending on our unique personalities or backgrounds. There is no formula or checklist because the Holy Spirit is a person. He is also God. He will provide comfort when we seek it from Him. We also know that our comfort is not just for us.

Read 2 Corinthians 1:3-4 and answer the following questions:

Who is the source of our comfort? (v. 3)

Why does God comfort us? (v. 4)

God is the source of our comfort, and He does it not only for our own sake but also so that we can comfort others.

Have you been able to comfort others after receiving God's comfort during a difficult season? If so, record some ways you gave comfort below:

Whether or not you can think of a time when you comforted someone else, you may be able to remember a time when someone comforted you. Write briefly how you were helped by another person during a tough time:

Today I've been texting with another godly woman who knows the same brand of pain I've been feeling. She walked through a very similar situation over five years ago. Because she had entrusted me with some of her story earlier in our relationship, I was able to reach out to her when I experienced something very similar. I didn't share many details but told her in vague terms, and she has been sending me prayers via text. Just knowing how things turned out in her situation gives me hope that something redemptive might be in our future. Having her prayers, receiving her texts, and knowing I am not alone gives me comfort. I know of others who have walked similar roads of infertility, divorce, illness, the loss of a child, or any myriad of difficult situations we might face. They were able to comfort one another from a place of empathy rather than merely sympathy. God comforts us and then gives us the precious gift of sharing His comfort with others.

Let's end our day of study with some Scriptures that highlight God's character as a Comforter.

Read the following verses and draw a star beside the one that resonates most with you today:

Lord, *you know the hopes of the helpless.*
   Surely you will hear their cries and comfort them.
                                    (Psalm 10:17)

When doubts filled my mind,
   your comfort gave me renewed hope and cheer.
                                    (Psalm 94:19)

My eyes are straining to see your promises come true.
   When will you comfort me?
                                    (Psalm 119:82)

God blesses those who mourn, for they will be comforted.
                                    (Matthew 5:4)

[16]**Now may our Lord Jesus Christ himself and God our Father, who loved us and by his grace gave us eternal** [17]**comfort and a wonderful hope, comfort you and strengthen you in every good thing you do and say.**
                                    (2 Thessalonians 2:16-17)

As you think of the Holy Spirit's role as a Comforter, maybe you are in need of comfort right now. If so, write below some of the things happening in your life that are annoying, painful, or even devastating:

Now write a prayer below asking the Holy Spirit to bring you comfort in your heart and mind:

Life can be so hard, but comfort comes from our Creator. We can press into our relationship with the Holy Spirit of God when we are looking for help to soothe our pain.

Behold

The Holy Spirit of God lives in us and will comfort us in times of trouble.

Believe

Write a statement of belief:

I don't need to look for comfort in _____
because I can turn to the Holy Spirit for help.

Bloom

Whether or not you are in a season where you are seeking comfort, you likely know someone who is. Take a moment to ask God's Spirit to bring to mind someone in your sphere of influence who is facing hard times. Maybe it is a family member, friend, neighbor, coworker, or person in your church. Ask the Lord to give you creative ideas of how you might bring this person comfort in his or her time of suffering.

Write any ideas that come to mind below:

We don't have to suffer alone. God has provided His own Spirit to bring us comfort for life's many woes. I am counting on His comfort in my life, and you can too!

Talk with God

Holy Spirit, thank You being my Advocate, Helper, and Comforter. Help me not to look for comfort in things that only provide fleeting relief. I don't want to numb myself, but instead allow You to heal my hurts. Show me what it looks like to receive Your kind of comfort as I face the realities in my life today. Amen.

Memory Verse Exercise

Read the Memory Verse on page 140 several times, and then fill in the blanks below as you recite it:

_____ _____ is _____, so _____ who _____ him _____ _____ in _____ _____ in _____.

(John 4:24)

Big Idea

We don't need something, we need Someone— the Holy Spirit of God—to comfort us in our troubles.

Weekly Wrap Up

Review the Big Idea for each day, and then write any personal application that comes to mind.

Day 1: Adonai—Master
Big Idea: Adonai is a loving Master to be obeyed, even when we have questions.

Personal Application:_____

_____

Day 2: Abba—Father
Big Idea: Jesus revealed the Father not as a ruling patriarch of His people but as Abba, a tender and gracious daddy.

Personal Application:_____

_____

Day 3: Ruwach—The Spirit of God
Big Idea: Although the Holy Spirit's roles in the Old and New Testaments aren't identical, His work remains consistent in empowering God's people.

Personal Application:_____

_____

Day 4: Holy Spirit—Teacher

Big Idea: God gave us the Holy Spirit to guide us when it comes to prayer, truth, and direction in life, so we want to be teachable students.

Personal Application:_____

_____

Day 5: Holy Spirit—Comforter

Big Idea: We don't need something, we need Someone—the Holy Spirit of God—to comfort us in our troubles.

Personal Application:_____

_____

Video Viewer Guide: Week 5

Romans 5:5*b*; 8:2, 6, 11

John 3:6-8

The Spirit of God has been enabling God's ________________ with God's ________________ from the very beginning.

We don't need something. We need ________________.

John 16:5-7

Ask ________________.

The Holy Spirit doesn't require our perfection, but He does require our participation.

Listen ______________________.

______________________.

Week 6

JESUS

*Savior, Messiah, Redeemer,
I AM, Name Above all Names*

Memory Verse

*Therefore, God elevated him to the place of highest honor
and gave him the name above all other names,
that at the name of Jesus every knee should bow,
in heaven and on earth and under the earth,
and every tongue declare that Jesus Christ is Lord,
to the glory of God the Father.*
(Philippians 2:9-11)

Day 1: Jesus—Savior

Pictures of Jesus hung on the walls of several of my Sunday school classes during my elementary school years. Some of them revealed images of a man who looked scrawny or even spooky; other pictures showed Him surrounded by sheep with a loving smile. Through the years, as my relationship with Jesus has grown, the images of Him that come to mind have developed and changed.

Scripture Focus

Matthew 1:18-25; Romans 6:4-14

What sort of pictures of Jesus do you remember from your childhood?

I asked this question to a few friends, and they mentioned that every picture they saw of Jesus when they were younger showed Him with long wavy hair. Another said He always wore a robe, sash, and sandals in pictures. Someone mentioned that He seemed to have a halo in the pictures they remembered. One person shared that her parents had a painting in their home with four children sitting at Jesus's feet.

Today when you think of Jesus, how do you picture Him?

Whether you see Jesus as He appears in a painting you've seen, imagine Him in a particular Bible story, or see Him as an infant in the manger, we know He cannot be fully captured with words or a paintbrush. Scripture reveals many names for Him so that we might have a well-developed understanding of His character. The more our minds know Him, the better our hearts can love Him. And the more we love Him, the more we know Him. In our final week together, we will look at some of the names of Jesus found in the Bible.

We begin with the name "Jesus." I have to admit that I've recently learned some things I never knew about His name. For example, the name "Jesus" has only been used for about four hundred years. Now we know that Jesus died over two thousand years ago, so what were His followers calling Him before that? We must go back to the original languages of the Bible to understand the etymological progression of Jesus's name. In Hebrew, His name is Yeshua, which essentially means "Yahweh is salvation."[1] In Greek, Jesus is *Iesous*.[2] The 1611 King James Bible uses the spelling *Iesus*, pronounced ee-ay-sooce.[3] The letter J wasn't introduced to the English language until the sixteenth century. It was during this time that English-speaking people began using the name Jesus to refer to the Savior.

The first mention of Jesus's name is found in the first verse of the New Testament. Matthew began his Gospel by establishing a genealogical link between Abraham and Jesus (Matthew 1:1-17), and then we find an explanation of how Jesus was named.

Read Matthew 1:18-25 and answer the following questions:

Who appeared to Joseph to instruct him about Jesus's name? (v. 20)

Why was the child to be called Jesus? (v. 21)

What other name for Jesus do we encounter here? (v. 23)

Joseph obeyed the angel's instructions and named the baby Jesus. It is fitting that we call Him Savior since, as we've seen, the name Jesus (Yeshua) essentially means "Yahweh is salvation."[5] He was born to save us from our sins by becoming the perfect sacrifice through His death and resurrection. We can't appreciate Jesus as a Savior until we recognize that we were in trouble and in need of being saved.

Take a moment to consider where you would be without Jesus. Write below a few thoughts regarding how your life would be different without Him:

One of the first things that comes to my mind is that I would not have hope for the future. John 3:16-17 says, "For this is how God loved the world: He gave his one and only Son, so that everyone who believes in him will not perish but have eternal life. God sent his Son into the world not to judge the world, but to save the world through him." My sin separated me from God, but through faith in Christ, I now live in the hope of life that will never end. Scripture describes this eternal state as a place where Christ will wipe every tear from our eyes because death, sorrow, crying, and pain will be gone forever

(Revelation 21:4). Jesus has saved me from the penalty of sin, which is eternal separation from God.

As I consider this life on earth, I also experience salvation from Jesus as He gives me power over sin. I'm battling it every day. My selfishness, laziness, and general bent toward wandering away from God cannot be overcome with willpower, a well-thought-out plan, or any sort of behavior modification technique. The power of Christ in me is saving me from sin as I yield to His Spirit living inside me.

Read Romans 6:4-14 and write a brief description of how Jesus is our salvation when it comes to our daily choices:

It is through Christ Jesus that we have power over sin. He longs for us to give up trying to fix ourselves and allow His grace and power to enable us to live new lives. None of us will ever be sinless in this life, but through Jesus's saving grace and power, we can sin less as we grow in faith.

If you are a follower of Christ, write a prayer below thanking Jesus for His salvation in your life:

I can't imagine my life without Jesus. He has given me peace, purpose in life, and hope in difficult times. I have many questions and doubts, but I know that without Him I would be utterly lost. I wonder if there are some things going on in your life right now where you are crying out to God for help. Perhaps you are battling fear, depression, or anxiety. Maybe you are grieving a loss or enduring a difficult relationship. I have cried out for God's rescue in smaller trials such as time management or food choices and also in deeper issues such as broken friendships or financial desperation.

Are you struggling with any small annoyances or deeper difficulties right now? If so, write about it below:

We need a Savior every day to deliver us from trials and empower us to turn away from sin.

Read the following Scriptures, noting the word *Savior* in each one. Put a star next to the verses that resonate most with you today:

Why am I discouraged?
    Why is my heart so sad?
I will put my hope in God!
    I will praise him again—
    my Savior and my God!
        (Psalm 42:11)

But as for me, I am poor and needy;
    please hurry to my aid, O God.
You are my helper and my savior;
    O Lord, do not delay.
                (Psalm 70:5)

[68]*"Praise the Lord, the God of Israel,*
    because he has visited and redeemed his people.
[69]*He has sent us a mighty Savior*
    from the royal line of his servant David,
[70]*just as he promised*
    through his holy prophets long ago.
                (Luke 1:68-70)

But we are citizens of heaven, where the Lord Jesus Christ lives. And we are eagerly waiting for him to return as our Savior.

                (Philippians 3:20)

This is why we work hard and continue to struggle, for our hope is in the living God, who is the Savior of all people and particularly of all believers.

                (1 Timothy 4:10)

[12]*And we are instructed to turn from godless living and sinful pleasures. We should live in this evil world with wisdom, righteousness, and devotion to God,* [13]*while we look forward with hope to that wonderful day when the glory of our great God and Savior, Jesus Christ, will be revealed.* [14]*He gave his life to free us from every kind of sin, to cleanse us, and to make us his very own people, totally committed to doing good deeds.*

                (Titus 2:12-14)

In light of these passages, what kind of active response should a believer have to Jesus's saving work in their lives? (Hint: Pay attention to the verbs.)

Some of the verbal phrases that stood out to me in these passages include:

- praise
- hope
- eagerly wait (for His return)
- work hard
- continue to struggle
- live with wisdom, righteousness, and devotion to God

Because Jesus is our Savior, we live with hope in the midst of our struggles. No portrait of Jesus can capture all that He has done to save us. The more we behold Him, the more we can believe Him. Then our lives can bloom with wonder at His salvation!

Behold

Jesus's name means "Yahweh is salvation," and He was born to save us from sin.

Believe

Write a statement of belief:

Jesus did not come to condemn me but to _____ me.

Because Jesus is my Savior, I am saved from _____ to walk in the freedom of His grace.

Bloom

As you reflect on Jesus's name and the Scriptures we studied today, what stands out most to you right now?

Do any new thought patterns, action steps, or life changes come to mind as you consider Jesus's saving work in your life?

End our time today by writing a sentence of praise for the Savior of the world who came to earth to rescue you from sin:

Talk with God

Jesus, You are my Savior. Without You, I am lost. Each day I recognize that I need You. Thank You for saving me from the penalty of sin. Lord, I want to live with power over sin, but I'm struggling. Help me to live by faith rather than try to fix myself. Amen.

Memory Verse Exercise

Read the Memory Verse on page 172 several times, and then fill in the blanks below as you recite it:

⁹**Therefore, _____ elevated him to the place of highest honor**

 and _____ him the name above all other names,

¹⁰**that at the _____ of Jesus every knee should bow,**

 in _____ and on earth and under the earth,

¹¹**and _____tongue declare that Jesus Christ is Lord,**

 to the _____ of God the Father.

(**Philippians 2:9-11**)

Big Idea

Jesus's name means salvation because He came to save us from our sins.

Scripture Focus

Matthew 16:13-16

Day 2: Jesus—Messiah

As a teenager I remember finding my identity in being an academic, a tennis player, the school mascot, and a Christian. Many of those defining factors have changed with time. (I haven't picked up a tennis racket in years!) Today I might refer to myself as a pastor's wife, a mother, a friend, an author, and a speaker, in addition to a follower of Christ. Our answers to the question "Who am I?" can be multifaceted.

What are some ways you would answer the question "Who am I?" in this season of life?

For those of us who consider ourselves followers of Christ, we answer the question of our identity in light of another question: "Who is God?" As we see Him more clearly, our own identities come into sharper focus. Jesus asked His disciples a question related to His identity.

Read Matthew 16:13-16. What two questions did Jesus ask?

1.

2.

What answer did Peter give to the second question?

How would you answer the question "Who do people say that Jesus is?"

This question is important for us as we navigate a pluralistic culture. Many people today will acknowledge Jesus as a moral figure, good teacher, or even someone worth emulating for his humility and love. Men such as John the Baptist, Elijah, and Jeremiah were moral teachers worthy of following, but Jesus was much more than a mere example. He is the Messiah, the fulfillment of every Old Testament prophecy of One who would come to restore the relationship broken by sin.

In Hebrew, the word *Messiah* is *Mashiyach* and means "anointed, anointed one."[6] Many scholars believe that the first hint of the the Jewish concept of a Messiah, an anointed one to come and deliver God's people, is found in Genesis 3:15 shortly after sin entered the world—referring to one who would strike the heel of the serpent (in other words, defeat Satan). Beginning there and continuing throughout the Old Testament, we find hints, shadows, and prophecies that point to a Messiah who would restore God's relationship with His creation.

The concept of anointing in ancient times involved smearing or rubbing oil on a person as part of a religious ceremony. For the Hebrews, anointing was linked to the offices of prophets, priests, and kings. All individuals who served in these offices were anointed with oil to signify that they were chosen of God.

Look up the following Old Testament verses and identify below which office each references: prophet, priest, or king.

Deuteronomy 18:15-16

1 Samuel 2:35

Zechariah 9:9

While a majority of Israelites did not believe that Jesus was the Messiah, many did embrace His fulfillment of prophecy. Anna and Simeon, who were at the temple when Jesus was born, prominent Jews who heard Jesus's teaching, such as Nicodemus and Joseph of Arimathea, and many common laborers, including the disciples and other followers, all believed.

Many Israelites were anticipating that a Messiah would come and deliver them. So why didn't more of them recognize Jesus as Messiah? It's possible that some lost sight of the passages regarding a humble, suffering servant and overlooked those prophecies that pictured the Messiah as prophet and priest, turning their focus to the references of a conquering king. One source notes, "The restoration of national glory was the great hope of Israel."[7] So it may be that by looking for a triumphant leader who would soothe their national and political woes, many missed God's revelation of Himself through Jesus. This is the grave danger of a limited view of God. We are studying God's names so that by looking at the whole counsel of Scripture, we do not narrow our understanding of Him.

The Messiah would be a conquering King, but He also would fulfill the role of a suffering servant. Christianity was born out of Judaism. In Christ we find fulfillment of all prophecies about Him. The Hebrew word *Messiah* is translated *Christos* in Greek; so, when we encounter the word *Christ* in the New Testament, it is a reference to Jesus as Messiah.[8]

Read in your Bible these New Testament passages to see how Christ fulfills the prophecies of the anointed offices of prophet, priest, and king. Then draw a line to match each Scripture with the correct office.

John 5:37-38	**King**
Hebrews 2:17	**Prophet**
Matthew 21:4-9	**Priest**

Jesus is the Messiah! Peter saw Him for who He was, and I hope we will as well. Jesus's fulfillment of each of the roles of prophet, priest, and king impacts our lives in tangible ways. Let's pause for a moment to bring these truths a little closer to home by considering three As.

Announce

Prophets spoke God's messages. Jesus is the very Word of God (John 1:1). We don't have to stumble through our lives wondering what God's message is for us. He announced it through Jesus, the final prophet.

What question would you want to ask Jesus if He were sitting next to you right now? Write anything that comes to mind below:

While you may not get a specific answer to your question, we can bring all of our questions to the One who proclaims God's message of hope, life, and forgiveness to us. We don't have to look any further for a prophet to guide us because we have Jesus.

Take a moment to thank Jesus for being God's mouthpiece so that we can find clarity and purpose through His guidance:

Access

The high priest was the mediator between God and His people. Jesus now gives us direct access to relationship with God (1 Timothy 2:5).

How can you more fully appreciate and utilize this access to God that Jesus provides?

I know that I can easily take for granted this precious gift. Reading through Leviticus reminds me of the complicated procedures for drawing near to God that involved blood and sacrifice and provided only temporary access. Jesus cut out the middleman and allows us to come boldly before the throne of grace (Hebrews 4:16).

Authority

Human kings led people to conquer other nations and provided stability and direction. Jesus is the King of kings (Revelation 19:16). He rules and reigns in our lives as we humbly serve Him as master.

How is Jesus calling you to submit more fully to His reign in your life?

I'm so grateful that Jesus is a good King. He loves us completely so we can yield to His rule without fear. We don't ever have to wonder if we got the wrong guy when it comes to His identity as Messiah.

Here are just a few other Old Testament messianic prophecies that were fulfilled by Christ. I'm listing the references in case you want to do some deeper study:

- He would be born of a virgin. (Isaiah 7:14; Luke 1:35)
- He would be born in Bethlehem. (Micah 5:2; Matthew 2:4-6)
- He would go to Egypt. (Hosea 11:1; Matthew 2:14-15)
- He would become the perfect sacrifice. (Psalm 40:6-8; Hebrews 10:5-10)
- He would teach with parables. (Psalm 78:1-2; Matthew 13:34-35)

- He would be a stone people would stumble over. (Isaiah 8:14; 1 Peter 2:7-8)
- His ministry would begin in Galilee. (Isaiah 9:1-2; Matthew 4:12-17)
- He would perform miracles. (Isaiah 35:5-6; Matthew 11:2-6)
- He would be despised and rejected. (Isaiah 53:3; Luke 4:28-29)
- He would be betrayed for thirty pieces of silver. (Zechariah 11:12-13; Matthew 27:6-10)
- He would be the Passover Lamb. (Exodus 12:21-27; 1 Corinthians 5:7)
- None of his bones would be broken. (Exodus 12:46; John 19:31-36)
- His hands and feet would be pierced. (Psalm 22:16; John 19:36-37)
- People would cast lots for his clothes. (Psalm 22:18; John 19:23-24)
- He would rise again. (Psalm 118:17-18; Luke 24:5-7)

This sampling is just the tip of the iceberg. Jesus fulfilled over three hundred prophecies to remove any question about His role as the promised Messiah.[9]

In light of all we have studied today, how would *you* answer Jesus's question, "Who do you say that I am?"

We might have a variety of answers because He is our Savior, Messiah, and so much more—as we will find throughout this week. We better understand the weight of Peter's answer that Jesus is Messiah when we understand the meaning of this name. Peter believed He was the anointed One of God who had been written about for centuries. Out of Peter's belief sprung a bold relationship with the Son of God. As we see Jesus as the Anointed Messiah sent from God, we see ourselves more clearly. Knowing that Christ is who He says He is, we can more boldly understand our own identities as those He came to save.

Behold

Jesus is the promised Messiah.

Believe

Write a statement of belief:

Jesus, because you are the Messiah, I believe you are _____

_____.

Bloom

We can't fully understand our own identity until we know the identity of our Maker. Our Abba Father sent His Son Jesus to deliver us from sin. He is Christ, the anointed One from heaven.

In response to today's study, what thoughts or questions come to mind?

I pray that seeing Christ's fulfillment of Old Testament prophecy gives deeper roots to your faith in Him. When we see Him more clearly, we can love Him more fully. Our identity can be found in our position as adopted children of the King of kings. We are His servants but also His dearly loved children. He died to fulfill His role as our Messiah, and we can live today in gratitude for His sacrifice.

Talk with God

Jesus Christ, You are the Son of the Living God. You are the promised Messiah and I believe by faith in your fulfillment of the Scriptures. You embody the anointed roles of prophet, priest, and king. Help me to see you clearly and serve You fully. I want to find my identity in Your plan for my life, knowing that my thoughts, attitudes, and actions flow out of my identity. Show me who You are and who I am so that I might bring You glory today. Amen.

Memory Verse Exercise

Read the Memory Verse on page 172 several times, and then fill in the blanks below as you recite it:

Big Idea

We can stand firm in our belief that Jesus is the promised Messiah that Scripture foretold.

⁹*Therefore, _____ elevated him to the _____ of highest honor*

    and _____ him the _____ above all other names,

¹⁰*that at the _____ of Jesus every _____ should bow,*

    in _____ and on _____ and under the earth,

¹¹*and _____ tongue declare that _____ Christ is Lord,*

    to the _____ of God the Father.

                                     (Philippians 2:9-11)

Day 3: Jesus—Redeemer

Over the years, my husband, Sean, and I have received many thoughtful gifts. At holidays or during pastor appreciation month, friends or church members have written us notes containing gift cards. I must admit that gift cards are my love language. They have provided a way for my husband and me to go on many dates when we wouldn't have been able to otherwise.

Scripture Focus

Hebrews 9:11-28

At one time, Sean had several gift cards in his Jeep that we planned to space out over the course of months. Because of some work we were doing in the garage, the vehicle was parked outside one particular night, and a thief broke into his Jeep and stole his wallet. While it was a pain to cancel his bank card and get a new driver's license, we mourned the loss of the gift cards the most. We could not enjoy them until they were redeemed.

In order to experience the benefit of the gift, those cards had to be received, revealed, and then redeemed. In the context of the Bible, redemption carries a much deeper meaning, but it is truly the most precious of gifts. The Hebrew word for "redeemer" is *gaal* and means "to redeem, act as kinsman-redeemer, avenge, revenge, ransom, do the part of a kinsman."[10] Redemption means to buy something back.

In the Old Testament, we find the concept of redemption using the word *gaal* over eighty times. Redemption happened when something was lost or broken and then restored. We find the name Redeemer used often in the Book of Job. Job was a man who lost his business, children, and health. He cried out to God as His Redeemer. Job expressed His faith as he prayed, "But as for me, I know that my Redeemer lives, and he will stand upon the earth at last" (Job 19:25).

The Book of Ruth is another place where redemption is highlighted. Naomi was a woman whose husband and sons died. She changed her name to Mara, which means bitter, to express all that she had lost. Redemption came for her family when a relative named Boaz married her foreign daughter-in-law Ruth and restored her family's land and name. Ruth also became pregnant with a child who was included in the Messianic lineage. "Then the women of the town said to Naomi, 'Praise the LORD, who has now provided a redeemer for your family! May this child be famous in Israel'" (Ruth 4:14).

A redeemer serves to buy back or restore what has been lost. What are some losses you have experienced in your life?

Extra Insight

A kinsman-redeemer had certain obligations to close relatives who had sold land or even themselves because of poverty. He was usually the nearest living male blood relative and could redeem the property and persons who had been sold.[11]

Some of us have lost jobs, loved ones, or our own health, but every person is lost in sin—separated from a holy God. After God created a perfect world, Adam and Eve disobeyed God and this brought about shame and separation. Sin brought a curse on the entire planet so that the inclination of every human heart became bent toward sin. This sin brought suffering, sickness, and ultimately death. Yet as we've considered, from the moment sin's curse fell, Yahweh had a plan to save His people (see the discussion of Genesis 3:15 on page 79). We've seen this week that Jesus is our Savior and Messiah, and today we will explore His position as Redeemer.

In the New Testament we find the Greek word *lutrosis* translated as "redeem" or "redemption." It means "a ransoming, redemption; a deliverance, esp. from the penalty of sin."[12] Zechariah was the first person to use this word in the New Testament when he prophesied,

> [68]"Praise the Lord, the God of Israel,
>   because he has visited and redeemed his people.
> [69]He has sent us a mighty Savior
>   from the royal line of his servant David,
> [70]just as he promised
>   through his holy prophets long ago."
>   (Luke 1:68-70)

Zechariah was the father of John the Baptist, who foretold the birth of Christ—a baby born not just to bring a message from God, but to die a criminal's death on a cross to redeem us. Through His shed blood, He restored our relationship with a Holy God. At times, I've wondered why blood, death, and sacrifice were needed to redeem our relationship with God. Have you ever had thoughts like that?

Read Hebrews 9:11-28 and answer the following questions:

How did Christ secure our redemption? (v. 12)

How is Christ's sacrifice described? (v. 14)

What did Christ's sacrifice set us free from? (v. 15)

What isn't possible without the shedding of blood? (v. 22)

What is destined for each person? (v. 27)

What will Christ not come to do when He returns? (v. 28)

What will He come to do? (v. 28)

What are some truths that stood out to you about Christ's role as a Redeemer?

I noticed that:

- the old system of animal sacrifice was temporary but Christ's sacrifice is eternal,
- animal sacrifices had to be repeated but Christ's offering was once and for all,
- blood is necessary for cleansing in God's economy, and
- Christ has set us free from the penalty of sin.

I've talked to individuals who believe there are many ways to God. My heart always wonders, if there were another way to save us, why would God allow His one and only Son to endure the cross? To say that it was painful and costly would be an understatement.

I was talking recently with some girlfriends about the movie *The Passion of the Christ*. We talked about how difficult it was to watch because it was so graphic and real, bringing the Scriptures to life. Jesus sweat blood in anticipation of what He knew He would endure (Luke 22:44). He was mocked (Mark 15:32), spat upon (Matthew 26:67), and beaten (John 19:1). A crown of thorns was placed upon His head (John 19:2). After Jesus carried the cross (John 19:17), He was nailed to it beside two criminals (Matthew 27:35). If there was any other way to redeem us, I would think God would have chosen it. Instead, Jesus was willing to pay the highest price for us. The animal sacrifices of the Old Testament provided shadows and hints. They were temporary measures pointing to the ultimate Redeemer who would come and give His life as the perfect sacrifice.

Let's look at a few more passages. Answer the questions following each one:

⁴But when the fullness of time had come, God sent forth His Son, born of a woman, born under the law, ⁵to redeem those who were under the law, that we might receive adoption as sons.

(Galatians 4:4-5 NKJV)

Who was to be redeemed?

What would they receive through this redemption?

⁷In him we have redemption through his blood, the forgiveness of our trespasses, according to the riches of his grace, ⁸which he lavished upon us, in all wisdom and insight.

(Ephesians 1:7-8 ESV)

Through what was redemption accomplished?

¹⁸For you know that you were not redeemed from your useless [spiritually unproductive] way of life inherited [by tradition] from your forefathers with perishable things like silver and gold, ¹⁹but [you were actually purchased] with precious blood, like that of a [sacrificial] lamb unblemished and spotless, the priceless blood of Christ.

(1 Peter 1:18-19 AMP)

What were we redeemed from?

After sin brought separation, Jesus bought us back through His blood. Once we understand what was lost through sin, we can appreciate more fully Christ's redemption. His work on the cross paid the price for sin so that we now have restored relationship with God. This is good news!

How does knowing that Christ is a Redeemer encourage you today?

I am encouraged when I think of Christ's forgiveness. We read in Hebrews that without the shedding of blood there is no forgiveness of sin. Christ's sacrifice paid the penalty for my sin, making God's forgiveness and freedom possible. This encourages me as I think about things I've said and done in the past that I wish I could take back. Knowing that Christ completely forgives me, I don't have to live in shame or regret. And neither do you! Hallelujah!

Forgiveness affects not only our past but also our present. In the flesh we are selfish, unkind, and lazy. We want to do what is right, but we struggle. God's forgiveness frees us, assuring us that we can repent and change because of God's grace and kindness—without fear of judgment. Our future is also marked by forgiveness. We can anticipate living in heaven with God through the forgiveness we receive through Christ. And all of this is possible not because of what we have done but because of our faith in what Jesus has done. Talk about freedom!

Sin leads the way to suffering and bondage, but redemption delivers us to a place of forgiveness and freedom. Knowing this, let us turn to our Redeemer rather than to worldly distractions whenever we experience loss and trouble.

Behold

Jesus has redeemed us through His blood shed on the cross.

Believe

Write a statement of belief:

Because Christ has paid the price for my sin, I _____

_____.

Bloom

Take a moment to relish the redemption that Christ's death and resurrection accomplished for you. Beholding and believing that Christ has redeemed you can help you remember to seek Him when you feel lost in life.

Write below any thoughts on how you can turn to Jesus for restoration rather than to temporary escapes such as media, food, or other people to soothe the aches in your soul:

We can live with gratitude and hope knowing that we have been redeemed. While I'm thankful for the thoughtful gift cards I've received, they don't compare in any way to the ultimate gift. The greatest gift isn't a card to be redeemed at a store or restaurant but the Redeemer Himself, and His name is Jesus!

Talk with God

Jesus, I recognize the high price You paid for my sin. You redeemed me through the cross. Help me not to lose sight of that in the midst of today's distractions. I want to live in the forgiveness and freedom You purchased through Your blood. You are my Redeemer, so help me to look to You rather than to counterfeits to fill the ache inside. Amen.

Big Idea

Even though sin separated us from God, we can live with gratitude and hope, knowing that we have been reconciled through Jesus, our Redeemer.

Memory Verse Exercise

Read the Memory Verse on page 172 several times, and then fill in the blanks below as you recite it:

⁹*Therefore, _____ elevated _____to the _____ of*
_____ honor
    and _____ him the _____ above _____ other _____,
¹⁰*that at the _____ of _____ every _____ should _____,*
    in _____ and on _____ and _____ the earth,

¹¹and _____ tongue _____ that _____ Christ is _____,
   to the _____ of _____ the Father.

(Philippians 2:9-11)

Day 4: Jesus—I AM

Sometimes there is a big difference between what others think of us and who we really are. When I first began serving on the Aspire Women's Events tour (a tour of one-night events that include worship, Bible teaching, and Christian comedy), I loved the opportunity to serve as part of a team. I stood in awe of how much this small group of Bible teachers, worship leaders, and comedians enjoyed serving Jesus together. We experienced long car rides, shared meals, and times of prayer as we prepared to use our gifts for God's glory. As the years passed, we continued to enjoy our work and began to appreciate how different we are. One night, one of the team members came up with a single word to describe each of us. She used words like *sassy*, *quirky*, *sweet*, and even *rambunctious*. We all laughed at the words she assigned us whether we thought they were accurate or not.

As we discussed in our first day of study this week, many people had opinions about Jesus, but today we will focus on who Jesus said He was. Jesus used a phrase we've heard God use before—I AM.

Can you recall one of the names of God we've studied that is defined by the two words I AM? If so, write it below:

Scripture Focus

John 14; 15

In weeks 3 and 4, we looked at the Yahweh names of God. God revealed Himself to Moses saying, "I AM WHO I AM. Say this to the people of Israel: I AM has sent me to you" (Exodus 3:14). Yahweh is "I AM," the Self-Existent One. The New Testament helps us see that Christ is also self-existent. He didn't come into being when He was born in Bethlehem as a baby. He existed from the beginning—not as a created being but as the Great I AM.

Read the following verses and write any phrases that identify Christ as existing long before the curtain lifted on the nativity story:

John 1:1-3:

Colossians 1:15-17:

Jesus was present and active in the creative process. He also holds everything together.

Jesus also used "I AM" to refer to Himself. Through this name He revealed more of His character so that we could know Him better.

Read the following passages and fill in each blank with the name Jesus attached to the words I AM:

John 6:35   I am _____.

John 8:12   I am _____.

John 10:7   I am _____.

John 10:11   I am _____.

John 11:25   I am _____.

John 14:6   I am _____.

John 15:1   I am _____.

Of these seven "I am" statements, which one resonates most with you today? Why?

Jesus is the bread of life. Bread provides the sustenance we need for life physically, but only Jesus can sustain us spiritually. Jesus is the light of the world. His light guides us through a dark world. Jesus is the gate for the sheep. Just as a shepherd often would lie down and become the gate of protection for his flock, Jesus protects His followers from predators. Jesus also is the good shepherd. He cares for His people and watches over them. Jesus is the resurrection and the life. Jesus is the source of all truth and the only way to a restored relationship with God. And Jesus is the true grapevine. Through Christ, we can bear fruit that will honor the Father.

Today I want to camp out on the last two statements that Jesus made, which both focus on our access to God through Christ.

Read John 14:1-4 and summarize Christ's message in your own words:

Jesus reminds us that He will return so that we can be with Him always. But the disciples He was speaking to in this passage had some questions.

How did Thomas respond to Christ's promises in John 14:5?

Thomas didn't nod and pretend he understood. He asked for more details. Jesus responded with an "I Am" statement that leaves no question about His role as Savior, Messiah, and Redeemer.

Write Jesus's words in John 14:6 below:

Jesus referred to Himself as the Way. Early Christ-followers referred to themselves as "followers of the Way" (Acts 9:2). This verse leaves no room for "another way" to God. Jesus is the only way to God.

I've noticed that several popular Christian authors today downplay Christ's exclusivity. When faced with the question, "Is Jesus the way to God?" it seems that some are answering with both yes and no. They intimate that many ways point toward the same God. I find this posture confusing. What about John 14:6? Why did Jesus say there was no other way to God if there was? Why would the Father send his Son to be crucified if we could just be kind or give to the poor to have complete access to God?

Jesus claimed to be *the* way to God. He provides salvation through the cross (Romans 5:8). He is also our high priest, providing direct access so that we can boldly approach God's throne (Hebrews 4:14-16). We are able to pray in His name (John 16:23). Through His blood we can overcome the enemy (Revelation 12:11). Scripture asserts that Jesus is *the* Way.

Jesus also claimed to be the truth. I can get so caught up in discerning the difference between truth and subtle distortions of it that I forget that the Truth is a person, and His name is Jesus. When I need to differentiate truth from lies, I can seek out the wisdom of Jesus. He embodies the truth about God.

If you know Jesus, how has He helped you sort out truth in your life?

Jesus's Word and His Spirit have been powerful sources of discernment for me. When I pray and study, He helps me to see truth from His vantage point because He is the Truth!

Now, what is the last thing Jesus said about Himself in John 14:6?

I am the _____.

Jesus said that *life* is found in Him. One of the "I am" statements in our list of seven is John 11:25: "Jesus told her, 'I am the resurrection and the life. Anyone who believes in me will live, even after dying.'" Through His sacrifice on the cross and then His resurrection, Jesus alone can enable us to live forever with God.

Jesus also wants to help us live our lives today. It is counterintuitive that we find life by losing it, yet Jesus modeled this. He died so that we might live. The apostle Paul wrote in Galatians 2:20, "My old self has been crucified with Christ. It is no longer I who live, but Christ lives in me. So I live in this earthly body by trusting in the Son of God, who loved me and gave himself for me."

How is the Lord calling you to die to self today so that you might live for His glory? Write anything that comes to mind in these categories:

Interactions with people you might encounter:

Decisions you will make:

Time management for the hours of your day:

Money you will spend:

Your thought life:

Other: _____

Jesus wants to live through us, but we have to die to our selfish ways first. Then we can abide in Him and experience His power. The next "I am" statement gives us greater insight into what this looks like.

Read John 15:1-8 and answer the following questions:

Identify the vine and the gardener. (v. 1)

V:

G:

What did Jesus say had already pruned and purified the disciples? (v. 3)

What did Jesus call his followers to do? (v. 4)

Apart from Jesus, what spiritual fruit are we able to produce? (v. 5)

What will happen if we remain connected to God and His words remain in us? (v. 7)

When we produce much fruit, what happens? (v. 8)

Jesus told a story to illustrate the importance of staying connected to Him, revealing that He is the source of our strength to produce godly living. I find it so easy to get off track in the Christian life and focus on "doing" rather than "being." This passage reminds us that we can spin our wheels with endless spiritual activity, but it will yield no real fruit if we are trying to do it in our own strength.

Jesus revealed that He is our source. Apart from Him, we can do nothing. But when we remain in Him, we can produce good fruit. The apostle Paul told the church at Galatia that when God controls our lives, the fruit produced will be related to the postures of our hearts. As we've seen previously in our study, the fruit of the Spirit includes attitudes and actions characterized by "love, joy, peace, patience, kindness, goodness, faithfulness, gentleness, and self-control" (Galatians 5:22-23).

What does remaining in Jesus look like—practically—for a believer today?

Take a moment to evaluate the fruit in your life. How do your heart postures reveal how connected you've been to the vine of Christ? Rather than writing your answer, just take a moment to consider how you are doing at abiding in Christ, the true vine.

I find that the work of the Christian life centers around words such as *yield*, *abide*, and *surrender*. In order to do these things, I need faith. To remain in Christ

Extra Insight

Parables were simple stories meant to center around single truths.

means to direct my thoughts, actions, and attitudes toward things that will grow my faith. For me, this includes things such as:

- gathering with other believers to worship;
- reading the Bible regularly and curiously, seeking to know God through His Word;
- spending time in prayer talking and listening to God;
- avoiding things that sabotage my faith through distraction or delusion; and
- spending time in God's creation appreciating His work.

Jesus calls us to remain in Him. How does this specifically resonate in your life today? You can star one of the options above or write a new idea below:

Here's the good news: Jesus *wants* us to stay connected to Him. His I AM names remind us that He doesn't call us to work harder but to lean in to a deeper connection with Him. I hope that the weight of doing things for God is lifted as you focus on being closer to Jesus. He doesn't only want us to be associated with Him but also to be truly connected.

Behold

Jesus revealed Himself as the Great I AM.

Believe

Write a brief statement of belief choosing one of the I AM statements we read today:

Jesus, I believe you are _____.
Please reveal this attribute of yours more fully to me so that I can trust you more!

Bloom

After reading about Jesus today, I hope you see yourself more clearly too. You are the one He died to save. Through Him, you know the way and the truth, and you experience His life. When you are connected to Him, you bear good fruit. Based on today's study, write a few "I am" statements regarding who you are because of who He is:

Because of who He is, I am _____.

Because of who He is, I am _____.

Because of who He is, I am _____.

Talk with God

Jesus, You are the way and the truth. My whole life is wrapped up in You. Help me to remember that You are the true vine. Show me what it means to remain in You in the midst of so many daily distractions. Give me a greater faith to live boldly out of Your power rather than my own. Amen.

Memory Verse Exercise

Read the Memory Verse on page 172 several times, and then fill in the blanks below as you recite it:

⁹_____, _____ elevated _____to the _____ of
_____ honor

and _____ him the _____ _____ _____ other _____,

¹⁰that at the _____ of _____ _____ _____ should
_____,

in _____ and on _____ and _____ the _____,

¹¹and _____tongue _____ that _____ _____ is
_____,

to the _____ of _____ the Father.

(Philippians 2:9-11)

Big Idea

Jesus is the Great I AM, and He doesn't call us to work harder but to lean into a deeper connection with Him.

Day 5: Jesus—Name above All Names

Can you believe we have come to our last day of study together? My prayer is that you feel a deeper intimacy with God through the study of His names. We've seen Jesus as Savior, Messiah, Redeemer, and the Great I AM. As we stay connected to Him, we will find greater power and victory in our lives. This is the reverse economy of the Christian life: victory comes through surrender! To find our lives, we must lay them down.

Read Philippians 2:1-11 and write below some of the attitudes of Jesus found in verses 6-8:

Jesus gave up divine privileges, humbling Himself in obedience. In verse 9 we find the word *therefore*. All my life I've heard preachers say that when we see that word, we should ask ourselves, "What is it there for?" As we focus on these

Scripture Focus

Philippians 2:1-11; 2 Corinthians 1:20

verses in Philippians 2, consider that it was humility that preceded an elevated position.

How do verses 9-11 describe the position and name that God bestowed upon Jesus?

Jesus's name is above all other names. That should cause us to pause after six weeks of focusing on some pretty incredible names! Jesus who made Himself lowest was exalted to the highest. As I type these words, I sense conviction in my soul. I want to follow the way of Jesus but struggle against the voices of our culture that incite us to elevate rather than humble ourselves.

In what ways could the Lord be calling you to take the humble posture of Christ in some of your current circumstances?

Maybe the Spirit nudged you about your marriage, work relationships, or a situation at church. Remember that humility doesn't reveal a lack of strength or entail becoming a doormat. Jesus could never be described as weak.

Read these verses from Paul's Letter to the Corinthians, and circle the word below that is repeatedly used to describe Christ.

[18]*As surely as God is faithful, our word to you does not waver between "Yes" and "No."* [19]*For Jesus Christ, the Son of God, does not waver between "Yes" and "No." He is the one whom Silas, Timothy, and I preached to you, and as God's ultimate "Yes," he always does what he says.* [20]*For all of God's promises have been fulfilled in Christ with a resounding "Yes!" And through Christ, our "Amen" (which means "Yes") ascends to God for his glory.*

(2 *Corinthians* 1:18-20)

Yes   No   Maybe

Paul called Jesus the divine Yes! He always does what He says He will do.

How does knowing that Jesus is "Yes and Amen" give you encouragement or direction in your life right now?

This passage in 2 Corinthians goes on to say that we can stand firm with God's power. In fact, in the next verses we find a rare instance in which all three members of the Trinity are referenced.

Read the following verse and then record the verbs associated with each member:

²¹*It is God who enables us, along with you, to stand firm for Christ. He has commissioned us,* ²²*and he has identified us as his own by placing the Holy Spirit in our hearts as the first installment that guarantees everything he has promised us.*

(2 Corinthians 1:21-22)

God _____ us to stand firm.

Christ has _____ us and _____ us as His own.

The Holy Spirit _____ everything Christ has promised.

We can stand firm in faith not because of who we are but because of our Triune God.

How does knowing that God enables, commissions, identifies, and guarantees encourage you today?

Where is the Lord calling you to stand firm right now?

Write a prayer below asking the Lord to remind you of His names as you seek to stand firm in the coming weeks and months:

Jesus is our Savior, Messiah, Redeemer, the Great I AM, and the Name above every other name!

We've covered a lot of ground in these six lessons focusing on God's names. I hope that as you continue to read and study God's Word, you will be on the lookout for God's names. They reveal truths that we want to sink deep in our souls as we answer life's biggest questions regarding who God is and who we are. I pray that you have not only gathered information about God but also have responded to His invitation to be known.

Since the first time I studied God's names all those years ago, there have been many times over the course of decades when a name of God would come to my mind to encourage and empower me. I want that so badly for you as well! There is power in knowing God's names. Isaiah 52:6 says, "But I will reveal my

Big Idea

Because Jesus's name is above every other name, we can stand firm in our faith, knowing that He is more than enough in our lives.

name to my people, and they will come to know its power. Then at last they will recognize that I am the one who speaks to them." As we finish our study, I pray we are only beginning to experience the power that God wants to reveal to us through His names!

Behold

Jesus's name is above every name, and in Him we find the divine Yes!

Believe

Write a statement of belief, choosing one of Jesus's names:

I believe that Jesus's name is _____, and through Him I _____.

Bloom

Because Jesus's name is above every other name, we can stand firm in our faith knowing that He is more than enough in our lives; and as we do, we will see more and more fruit in our lives!

Instead of a Weekly Wrap-up, let's end our study by reviewing what we have learned throughout our weeks together.

Read through the main themes in the summary chart, and then draw a star beside the week that resonates most strongly with you during this season of your life. (Don't worry about the reflection questions yet, we will get to those later.)

Week of Study	Main Themes	Reflection Questions
1. Hashem, Elohim, El Elyon, El Roi	1. Our desire is not to misuse God's name but to worship the One who bears it. 2. Elohim created us, and He only makes good things. 3. Elohim is stronger than any problems we face today. 4. We can be delivered because we know the Deliverer, and His name is El Elyon, God Most High. 5. I am never alone because El Roi is the God who sees me.	How have you noticed the use or misuse of God's name since starting this study? What elements of Elohim's creation can you appreciate today? When you compare today's problems with Elohim's power, how does that encourage you? Is there anything you are seeking to be delivered from right now? Ask El Elyon for rescue—He is a Deliverer! Envision yourself right now as seen by God. How does knowing God as El Roi assure you of God's presence today?

Week of Study	Main Themes	Reflection Questions
2. El Shaddai, El Olam, El-Elo-he-Israel, El Chay	1. When we recognize El Shaddai's sufficiency, we can pursue greater dependency. 2. We can wait patiently knowing that El Shaddai will fulfill every promise He has made. 3. We live within the framework of time and look to El Olam to help us manage it wisely. 4. The Mighty God of the Universe is also the God of me. 5. We can cling to the presence and power of El Chay, the Living God, rather than look for quick fixes during dark seasons.	What are some things that seem to be lacking in your life currently? How can you lean into El Shaddai with greater dependency today? How does knowing that God will keep every promise He has made on His timetable help you wait with greater patience and expectation? El Olam is the everlasting God. How can you implement a more eternal perspective when it comes to your schedule and routines? Jacob discovered that God was His God. How has your study of God's names helped you to interact with the Lord in a more personal way? Knowing that God is El Chay, the Living God, where can you acknowledge God's activity and presence in daily life?
3. Yahweh Elohim, Yahweh, Yahweh Yireh, Yahweh Rapha, Yahweh Nissi	1. Yahweh never changes, and the name Yahweh Elohim highlights God's personal relationship with us. 2. Yahweh needs nothing from an outside source and has no beginning or end. 3. Yahweh Yireh sees our needs and provides resources, people, and information according to His timetable for our ultimate good rather than our immediate pleasure. 4. Yahweh Rapha longs for each of us to experience ultimate healing. 5. Yahweh Nissi's name reminds us that when we are weary, we can focus on the amazing things God has done in the past to give us strength in the present.	How does seeing God as Yahweh, the Self-Existent One, help you know Him more? What are some needs you currently have that you can bring before Yahweh Yireh in prayer? How is your view of God as a Healer strengthened or deepened through our study of Yahweh Rapha? Yahweh Nissi's name was revealed when Moses's friends held his arms up during battle. What are some things the Lord has done in the past that give you strength and hope for any current battles?

Week of Study	Main Themes	Reflection Questions
4. Yahweh Shalom, Yahweh Sabaoth, Yahweh Raah, Yahweh Tsidkenu, Yahweh Shammah	1. We don't create peace; we receive it from Yahweh Shalom. 2. We can find strength in life's battles as we trust Yahweh Sabaoth, the Lord of Heaven's Armies. 3. Yahweh Raah wants to lovingly shepherd His people and offers contentment, restoration, guidance, and protection. 4. Yahweh Tsidkenu is righteousness, and He makes us righteous through Christ. 5. Freedom is found in God's presence, Yahweh Shammah.	Where is the Lord calling you to rest in His peace? What battles are you facing lately? How does knowing that God is the Lord of Heaven's Armies encourage you in those battles? How can you respond to the Good Shepherd's leadership as He offers guidance and protection in your life? Where is the Lord calling you to stop striving to be righteous and instead lean into His righteousness? Take some time to reflect on God's promise to be there in your life. He is Yahweh Shammah.
5. Adonai, Abba, Ruwach, Holy Spirit	1. Adonai is a loving master to be obeyed even when we have questions. 2. Jesus revealed the Father not as a ruling patriarch of His people but as Abba, a tender and gracious daddy. 3. Although the Holy Spirit's roles in the Old and New Testaments aren't identical, His work remains consistent in empowering God's people. 4. God gave us the Holy Spirit to guide us when it comes to prayer, truth, and direction in life, so we want to be teachable students. 5. We don't need something, we need Someone—The Holy Spirit of God—to comfort us in our troubles.	What questions are you wrestling with in life right now? How can knowing God as Adonai help you trust and obey in spite of your questions? How is your view of God influenced by your relationship with your earthly Father? How does seeing God as Abba, Daddy, bring you comfort and safety? What qualities of the Holy Spirit stood out to you from our study? How is the work of the Holy Spirit different and similar in the Old and New Testaments? Where is the Lord calling you to take a more teachable posture in learning from the Holy Spirit? How has the Holy Spirit brought you comfort in the past? Where do you need comfort in your life currently?

Week of Study	Main Themes	Reflection Questions
6. Jesus—Savior, Messiah, Redeemer, I AM, Name Above all Names	1. Jesus's name means salvation because He came to save us from our sins. 2. We can stand firm in our belief that Jesus is the promised Messiah that Scripture foretold. 3. Even though sin separated us from God, we can live with gratitude and hope knowing that we have been reconciled through Jesus, our Redeemer. 4. Jesus is the Great I AM, and He doesn't call us to work harder but to lean into a deeper connection with Him. 5. Because Jesus's name is above every other name, we can stand firm in our faith knowing that He is more than enough in our lives.	How has knowing Jesus changed your life? How does knowing that Jesus fulfills Old Testament prophecy as Messiah strengthen your faith? How have you seen Jesus redeem difficult situations in your life and use them for good? Where is the Lord calling you to a more consistent connection with Him so that you stay connected to the True Vine? How do hope and peace come as you recognize Jesus as the name above every name and as the divine Yes?

How do the names of God in the week that you starred echo into your current circumstances?

Now write a few brief responses to the reflection questions listed for that week (right column of the chart):

As we turn the last page of our study together, let's remember that our mandate as followers of Jesus is not to try harder. We have focused each day on beholding, believing, and then allowing God to produce the blooms in our lives. I pray these progressions have renewed our minds with rich truths about God's character so that we can grow in faith and stand firm through all the ups and downs of daily life. Our challenge as we end our study is to "press on" in our pursuit to know our Creator!

Talk with God

Elohim, Yahweh, Adonai, Abba, Holy Spirit, Jesus…we worship You. We long to know You more. Help us to continue beholding You through Your Word, Your creation, and Your names. We want to believe You more and allow You to produce good fruit in our lives. Amen.

Memory Verse Exercise

Read the Memory Verse on page 172 several times, and then fill in the blanks below as you recite it:

9 _____, _____ _____ _____ *to the* _____ *of*

_____ _____

and _____ *him the* _____ _____ _____ _____

_____,

10 *that at the* _____ *of* _____ _____ _____ _____

_____,

in _____ *and on* _____ *and* _____ *the* _____,

11 *and* _____ _____ _____ *that* _____ _____ *is*

_____,

to the _____ *of* _____ *the* _____.

                                                    (Philippians 2:9-11)

Video Viewer Guide: Week 6

Pursuing wholeness requires a willingness to _____ _____.

Matthew 13:44-46

Pursuing wholeness means clinging to the _____ _____.

Christ fulfills the prophecies of the anointed offices of prophet, priest, and king.

Pursuing wholeness requires getting things in the _____ _____.

Matthew 6:33

Philippians 2:9-11

THE NAMES OF GOD
QUICK REFERENCE GUIDE

1. Hashem: The Name
2. Elohim: Strong Creator
3. El Elyon: God Most High
4. El Roi: The God Who Sees Me
5. El Shaddai: All-Sufficient One
6. El Olam: Everlasting God
7. El-Elohe-Israel: The God of Me (Israel)
8. El Chay: Living God
9. Yahweh: The Self-Existent One
10. Yahweh Yireh: The Lord Will Provide
11. Yahweh Rapha: The Lord Who Heals You
12. Yahweh Nissi: The Lord Our Banner
13. Yahweh Shalom: The Lord Is Peace
14. Yahweh Sabaoth: The Lord of Heaven's Armies
15. Yahweh Raah: The Lord My Shepherd
16. Yahweh Tsidkenu: The Lord Is Our Righteousness
17. Yahweh Shammah: The Lord Is There
18. Adonai: Master
19. Abba: Father
20. Ruwach: The Spirit of God
21. Holy Spirit: Teacher and Comforter
22. Jesus: Yahweh Saves
23. Messiah: Anointed One

Video Viewer Guide Answers

Introductory Video
better / better
Behold
Believe
Bloom
essential picture
El
Yahweh
Trinity
salvation
trust
glory

Week 1
cares / you
big picture
details

Week 2
sufficiency / dependency
relationship
provision
mercy
blessing

Week 3
past / present
vertical
vision
vulnerabilities

Week 4
peace / receive
peace
worship / worry

Week 5
people / power
Someone
expectantly
attentively
Surrender

Week 6
let go
right One
right order

NOTES

Week 1

1. Bible Study Tools, s.v. "Yisra'el," https://www.biblestudytools.com/lexicons/hebrew/kjv/yisrael.html, accessed April 3, 2020.
2. Merrill F. Unger, *The New Unger's Bible Dictionary* (Chicago: Moody Press, 1988), 903.
3. Tony Evans, *The Power of God's Names* (Eugene, OR: Harvest House Publishers, 2014), 12.
4. Ann Spangler, *The Names of God: 52 Bible Studies for Individuals and Groups* (Grand Rapids, MI: Zondervan, 2009), 77–79.
5. Bible Study Tools, s.v. *"shav',"* https://www.biblestudytools.com/lexicons/hebrew/nas/shav.html, accessed April 3, 2020.
6. Evans, *The Power of God's Names*, 19.
7. Derek Thomas, "Creation Ex Nihilo," https://www.ligonier.org/learn/articles/creation-ex-nihilo/, accessed April 4, 2020.
8. Andrew Jukes, *The Names of God: Discovering God as He Desires to Be Known* (Grand Rapids, MI: Kregel Publications, 1967), 16.
9. Spangler, *The Names of God*, 13.
10. Kay Arthur, *Lord, I Want to Know You: A Devotional Study on the Names of God* (Colorado Springs, CO: Waterbrook Press, 2000), 9.
11. Bible Study Tools, s.v. "'elohiym," https://www.biblestudytools.com/lexicons/hebrew/nas/elohiym.html, accessed April 4, 2020.
12. Paul Sumner, "'Elohim' in Biblical Context," Hebrew Streams, http://www.hebrew-streams.org/works/monotheism/context-elohim.html accessed April 4, 2020.
13. Alec Motyer, "What Is Progressive Revelation?" https://www.crossway.org/articles/what-is-progressive-revelation/, May 26, 2018.
14. Dictionary.com, s.v. "transcendent," https://www.dictionary.com/browse/transcendent, accessed April 4, 2020.
15. Evans, *The Power of God's Names*, 29.
16. Lester Sumrall, *The Names of God: God's Names Bring Hope, Healing, and Happiness* (New Kensington, PA: Whitaker House, 1982), 71.
17. Evans, *The Power of God's Names*, 178.
18. David Jeremiah, *My Heart's Desire: Living Every Moment in the Wonder of Worship* (Nashville: Integrity Publishers, 2002), 63.
19. Evans, *The Power of God's Names*, 177.
20. Unger, *The New Unger's Bible Dictionary*, 832.
21. Bible Study Tools, s.v. "Qalal," https://www.biblestudytools.com/lexicons/hebrew/nas/qalal.html, accessed April 4, 2020.

Week 2

1. Bible Study Tools, s.v. "Shadday," https://www.biblestudytools.com/lexicons/hebrew/nas/shadday.html, accessed April 4, 2020.
2. Arthur, *Lord, I Want to Know You*, 37.
3. Jukes, *The Names of God*, 74.
4. Merriam-Webster, s.v. "sufficient," https://www.merriam-webster.com/dictionary/sufficient, accessed April 4, 2020.
5. Bible Study Tools, "Abram," https://www.biblestudytools.com/lexicons/hebrew/nas/abram.html, accessed April 4, 2020.
6. Bible Study Tools, "Abraham," https://www.biblestudytools.com/lexicons/hebrew/nas/abraham.html, accessed April 4, 2020.
7. Spangler, *The Names of God*, 21.

8. Unger, *The New Unger's Bible Dictionary*, 259.
9. Bible Study Tools, "Shadday," https://www.biblestudytools.com/lexicons/hebrew/kjv/shadday.html, accessed April 4, 2020.
10. Unger, *The New Unger's Bible Dictionary*, 1252.
11. Jukes, *The Names of God*, 137.
12. Unger, *The New Unger's Bible Dictionary*, 310.
13. Bible Study Tools, "El-Elohe-Israel," https://www.biblestudytools.com/encyclopedias/isbe/el-elohe-israel.html, accessed April 4, 2020.
14. Behind the Name, s.v. "Israel," https://www.behindthename.com/name/israel, accessed April 4, 2020.
15. Evans, *The Power of God's Names*, 195.
16. Evans, *The Power of God's Names*, 195.

Week 3

1. Frank E. Gaebelein, *The Expositor's Bible Commentary Volume 2: Genesis, Exodus, Leviticus, Numbers* (Grand Rapids, MI: Zondervan, 1990), 323.
2. Bible Study Tools, s.v. "God, Names of," https://www.biblestudytools.com/dictionaries/bakers-evangelical-dictionary/god-names-of.html, accessed April 4, 2020.
3. Evans, *The Power of God's Names*, 51.
4. Spangler, *The Names of God*, 33.
5. Alistair Begg and Sinclair B. Ferguson, *Name above All Names* (Wheaton, IL: Crossway, 2013), 20.
6. Alyssa Roat, "What Is the Tetragrammaton? Meaning and Usage," Christianity.com, https://www.christianity.com/wiki/christian-terms/what-is-the-tetragrammaton-meaning-and-usage.html, accessed April 4, 2020.
7. Spangler, *The Names of God*, 35.
8. Arthur, Lord, *I Want to Know You*, 55.
9. Arthur, Lord, *I Want to Know You*, 67.
10. Spangler, *The Names of God*, 28.
11. Spangler, *The Names of God*, 29–30.
12. Bible Study Tools, s.v. "Rapha'," https://www.biblestudytools.com/lexicons/hebrew/nas/rapha.html, accessed April 4, 2020.
13. Gaebelein, *The Expositor's Bible Commentary Volume 2*, 399.
14. Gaebelein, *The Expositor's Bible Commentary Volume 2*, 399.
15. David Guzik, "Exodus 17—God's Provision and Protection of Israel," Enduring Word, https://enduringword.com/bible-commentary/exodus-17/, accessed April 4, 2020.

Week 4

1. "What Is Stress?" The American Institute of Stress, adapted from Daniel L. Kirsch and Michel A. Woodbury, "Stress in Health and Disease," *Psychiatric Clinics of North America* 37, no. 4 (2014), https://www.stress.org/daily-life, accessed April 4, 2020.
2. Bible Study Tools, s.v. "Shalowm," Bible Study Tools, https://www.biblestudytools.com/lexicons/hebrew/nas/shalowm.html, accessed April 4, 2020.
3. Bible Study Tools, s.v. "Tsaba'," https://www.biblestudytools.com/lexicons/hebrew/kjv/tsaba-2.html, accessed April 4, 2020.
4. Bible Study Tools, s.v. "Ra'am," https://www.biblestudytools.com/lexicons/hebrew/nas/raam-2.html, accessed April 4, 2020.
5. *The Woman's Study Bible, Second Edition*, NKJV (Nashville: Thomas Nelson, 2006), 355.
6. Spangler, *The Names of God*, 66.
7. John F. Walvoord and Roy B. Zuck, *The Bible Knowledge Commentary: Old Testament* (Wheaton, Il: Victor Books, 1985), 811.
8. Phillip Keller, *A Shepherd Looks at Psalm 23* (Grand Rapids, MI: Zondervan, 2015), 7.
9. Keller, *A Shepherd Looks at Psalm 23*, 7.
10. Keller, *A Shepherd Looks at Psalm 23*, 16.
11. Keller, *A Shepherd Looks at Psalm 23*, 24.
12. Keller, *A Shepherd Looks at Psalm 23*, 25.
13. Keller, *A Shepherd Looks at Psalm 23*, 31.
14. Keller, *A Shepherd Looks at Psalm 23*, 48.
15. Keller, *A Shepherd Looks at Psalm 23*, 59.
16. Keller, *A Shepherd Looks at Psalm 23*, 81.
17. Spangler, *The Names of God*, 8.

18. Bible Study Tools, s.v. "Tsedeq," https://www.biblestudytools.com/lexicons/hebrew/nas/tsedeq.html, accessed April 4, 2020.
19. Dave Wilkenson, "Prisoner of His Appetite," https://bible.org/illustration/prisoner-his-appetite, accessed April 4, 2020.
20. Brother Lawrence, *The Practice of the Presence of God* (New Kensington, PA: Whitaker House, 1982), 55.

Week 5

1. Jukes, *The Names of God*, 111.
2. Jukes, *The Names of God*, 115.
3. Jukes, *The Names of God*, 110.
4. Evans, *The Power of God's Names*, 56.
5. Unger, *The New Unger's Bible Dictionary*, 2.
6. Walter A. Elwell, "Fatherhood of God," Bible Study Tools, https://www.biblestudytools.com/dictionaries/bakers-evangelical-dictionary/fatherhood-of-god.html, accessed April 4, 2020.
7. Unger, *The New Unger's Bible Dictionary*, 2.
8. "Hebrew Word Study—Father," http://livingwordin3d.com/discovery/2016/10/17/hebrew-word-study-father/, accessed April 4, 2020.
9. Bible Study Tools, s.v. "Ruwach," https://www.biblestudytools.com/lexicons/hebrew/nas/ruwach-2.html, accessed April 4, 2020.
10. Bible Study Tools, s.v. "Ruwach," https://www.biblestudytools.com/lexicons/hebrew/kjv/ruwach-2.html, accessed April 4, 2020.
11. Charles Stanley, *The Wonderful Spirit-filled Life* (Nashville: Thomas Nelson, 1992), 31.
12. Bible Study Tools, s.v. "Parakletos," https://www.biblestudytools.com/lexicons/greek/nas/parakletos.html, accessed April 4, 2020.
13. Bible Study Tools, s.v. "Jesus Speaks of Both His Relation to the Father and His Disciples' Relation to the Father (14:8-21)," https://www.biblegateway.com/resources/ivp-nt/Jesus-Speaks-Both-Relation, accessed April 4, 2020.

Week 6

1. Chris Poblete, "Yahweh Is Salvation," https://blogs.blueletterbible.org/blb/2012/01/31/yahweh-is-salvation/, accessed April 4, 2020.
2. Bible Study Tools, "Iesous," https://www.biblestudytools.com/lexicons/greek/nas/iesous.html, accessed April 4, 2020.
3. King James Bible Online, "Matthew Chapter 1 (Original 1611 KJV Bible)," https://www.kingjamesbibleonline.org/Matthew-Chapter-1_Original-1611-KJV/, accessed April 4, 2020.
4. Spangler, 210–11.
5. "How 'Yeshua' Became 'Jesus,'" https://jesusisajew.org/YESHUA.php, accessed April 4, 2020.
6. Bible Study Tools, "Mashiyach," https://www.biblestudytools.com/lexicons/hebrew/nas/mashiyach.html, accessed April 4, 2020.
7. Unger, *The New Unger's Bible Dictionary*, 840.
8. Bible Study Tools, "Christos," https://www.biblestudytools.com/lexicons/greek/nas/christos.html, accessed April 4, 2020.
9. "Biblical Prophecies Fulfilled by Jesus," CBN, https://www1.cbn.com/biblestudy/biblical-prophecies-fulfilled-by-jesus, accessed April 4, 2020.
10. Bible Study Tools, "Ga'al," https://www.biblestudytools.com/lexicons/hebrew/nas/gaal.html, accessed April 4, 2020.
11. Unger, *The New Unger's Bible Dictionary*, 742.
12. Bible Study Tools, "Lutrosis," https://www.biblestudytools.com/lexicons/greek/nas/lutrosis.html, accessed April 4, 2020.